LIFE beyond DEATH

LIFE *beyond* DEATH

NORMAN VINCENT PEALE

A Giniger Book

ZondervanPublishingHouse
Grand Rapids, Michigan

A Division of HarperCollins*Publishers*

Life Beyond Death
Copyright © 1996 by The Norman Vincent Peale Trust

Requests for information should be addressed to:

🏭 ZondervanPublishingHouse
Grand Rapids, Michigan 49530

Library of Congress Cataloging-in-Publication Data

Peale, Norman Vincent, 1898-1994.
   Life beyond death / Norman Vincent Peale.
      p. cm.
      ISBN: 0-310-20908-0 (hardcover : alk. paper)
    1. Heaven—Christianity. 2. Future life—Christianity. I. Title.
BT846.2.P43   1996
263'.25—dc20
                                               96-32562
                                                CIP

This edition printed on acid-free paper and meets the American National Standards Institute Z39.48 standard.

Published in association with The K. S. Giniger Company, Incorporated, Publishers, 260 West 57th Street, #519, New York, NY 10107.

Interior design by Sue Vandenberg Koppenol

Printed in the United States of America

96 97 98 99 00 01 02 03/❖ QF/ 10 9 8 7 6 5 4 3 2 1

CONTENTS

Foreword

From the time Norman Vincent Peale began his career as a preacher in 1921 until his death on Christmas Eve 1994, he preached thousands of sermons, wrote hundreds of newspaper columns, contributed dozens of magazine articles, gave innumerable lectures, speeches, and radio and television talks. He became known internationally for his many popular books.

The bulk of this material, much of it never published in book form, is preserved at the Peale Center for Christian Living, in Pawling, New York. This makes it possible for his message to continue to go out in new and different forms.

Death, immortality, and the life beyond were among his many subjects and, of course, his sermons, newspaper columns, and magazine articles at Eastertide, in particular, concerned themselves with these themes.

I can still see Norman preaching Easter Sunday in Marble Collegiate Church on Fifth Avenue in New York, where he served for so many years—the church beautifully decorated with the white lilies a Bermuda friend had sent—and quoting what he believed were the greatest and most beautiful words ever spoken: "I am the resurrection, and the life: he that believeth in me, though he were dead, yet shall he live: And whosoever liveth and believeth in me shall never die."

You will find that those words, as well as others from the Bible, (which he made the touchstone of his thinking) are constantly repeated in this book . And he was able to face the loss of beloved ones—grandmother, mother, father, brothers, friends—with the certainty that he would see them again.

He describes his own experiences, as well as the experiences of many others, in the pages that follow. He was sure of life beyond death and of heaven (although he hoped he would not have to spend eternity playing the harp), where he knew he would find his loved ones waiting for him.

I, too, am sure of these things and I know that, somewhere out there, Norman is waiting for me.

In putting these words of Norman's into this form, I am grateful for the help of my assistant at the Peale Center, Sybil Light, who served as Norman's secretary for many years, and Kenneth Giniger, his longtime editor and publisher.

Ruth Stafford Peale
The Hill Farm
Pawling, New York

O N E

THE END OF TEARS

One of the profound sorrows of this world is the loss by death of our loved ones. It is a universal grief, for everywhere the funeral cortege winds solemnly to God's acre. No day passes but human minds wistfully ask the question, "Will we meet our loved ones again?"

One tragic night, eighty-four years ago, a mighty ship was crossing the North Atlantic. It was her maiden voyage. She was the pride of Britain's fleet, the greatest ship afloat. Her name was *Titanic*. Parties were in progress. Laughter and music floated out over the starlit waters. Everyone was happy. The magic of the silver moonlight turned the water into phosphorescence. The great engines throbbed steadily on as, with lights ablaze, the noble vessel glided through calm seas. Gradually the air grew chill, but those on deck thought it only the freshness of a spring night. Suddenly a dark green thing of terrifying size loomed dead ahead in the path of the ship. Vainly bells rang. The steersman put the wheel hard over, but no power on earth could stop that momentum or avoid the crash. There was no escape.

Then came scenes of immortal heroism. The innate nobility of human beings facing eternity was proved once again. The ship's lights went out, and on her slanting decks hundreds were hushed by the solemn strains of the band playing "Nearer, My God, to Thee." This story, one of the most tragic in the experience of our time, brings to mind the solemn philosophy of Charles Frohman, who, on the deck of the sinking *Lusitania*, said to a group of friends: "Why fear death? Death is only a beautiful adventure."

To be proficient in the art of living, we must know somewhat about dying, for, strangely enough, dying is an important factor in living. Death, we believe, is but a stage in life, a change into a different form of existence—like a caterpillar changing into a butterfly or a door opening into a larger life. In a world of wonders, the possibility of life after death grows apace.

It is remarkable how dogmatic and unscientific some scholars can become at times. For example, the British scientist who, some years ago, said, "At death the spirit of man will be extinguished like a candle flame." Of course, the question is, "How does he know that? Where is his evidence?" The plain fact is that he knows nothing about it, for, as Shakespeare pointed out, he is dealing with "the undiscovered country from whose bourne no traveler returns." Scientists like him are now rather out of date, for the greater scientific men tend to reset theism and more spiritual thinking at the center of their explanations about the universe and though, manifestly, they have not proven it and perhaps cannot categorically do so, their thinking is in the direction of faith in immortality.

It is natural that we should have an insatiable curiosity concerning the afterlife. When Henry Thoreau lay dying at Concord, his friend, Parker Pillsbury, sat by his side and said, "Henry, you are so near to the border now, can you see anything on the other side?" To which Thoreau, with a feeble smile, replied, "One world at a time, Parker." This may have been satisfying to the reflective mind of the sage of Walden Pond, but men do look with longing into that other land where their loved ones have gone. They have watched them go like ships, disappearing down the bay. They have stood and watched as they sailed into the great unknown and have asked, "Shall we meet our loved ones again?" The desire is a very normal one. In the long course of the years human lives grow close together. The sound of a voice becomes precious—the touch of a hand, the pressure of a step, the silent presence is a benediction. Here are a husband and wife, beloved companions of a long journey—will they meet again? Here also mother and father, sons and daughters, bound together in the tender relationship of a family. Mother and father grow old and fade back into the dust, leaving heartbreak and a sense of loneliness and longing in the hearts of children, where they will be cherished as long as life shall last. Will they see those dear faces again in some happier country?

There is nothing in this world as inexorable as time. "Change and decay in all around we see." Nothing remains as it is. Recently I revisited a little town in Ohio where, as a boy, I spent many happy summers at the home of my grandparents. I walked the old familiar streets, noting that houses, great to my once childish eyes, were now small and unimpressive, and I contemplated solemnly the evidences of change everywhere. I missed many people who once were prominent citizens of the place, but who had joined that ever-moving and innumerable caravan, which had gone over the hill into the sunset. Many whom I had known in the vigor of their lives were now broken and bowed with the weight of years.

I came finally to the home of a beloved aunt, where I had played with my cousins and my brothers in days long gone. I visited the old-fashioned barn, to me happily unchanged, and the haymow, once a place of mystery. I passed through the kitchen and into a pantry where hungry boys never failed to find the most delicious cookies in the state of Ohio, always awaiting us in a jar conveniently placed. But the hands that made them and the voice that sang about her work were gone, and the place was sad and strangely empty, for what is a house when the dear personalities which made it a home are gone?

But the high spot of my visit was when I rounded the corner of the house and found to my delight that the thing for which I was looking was still there. It was an old-fashioned swing, with opposite seats and made of metal. Well do I remember when, bright and shiny, it was set up for the first time. We boys played railroad train in it. I always wanted to be the conductor so that I could take up the money—only it was not money, but pins, I believe. But that was all long ago. Now the old swing will no longer swing. The platform has broken loose and rests on the ground. No longer is it bright and shiny, but rusty and frail. Touching it made it weave precariously. Time, I reflected, has done this—time, which makes everything old and frail. Time, which works this havoc with things, does it also to people, and, one by one, I knew that those I love would go from me.

Is this the end of all our happy associations? Everywhere the question intrudes upon our minds in poignant wistfulness, "Shall we meet our loved ones after death?" I believe that we shall; I am sure that we shall. There is no shadow of a doubt about it in my mind, but I cannot prove it for the skeptical mind. I cannot prove it any more than another can disprove it. You cannot prove a thing like this as you can a diagram in geometry or a case at law. There is no method by which it can be either proved or disproved. You simply know a truth like this by faith. Something whispers it to your heart in the form of a deep intuition or conviction. I could, of course, work out a satisfactory philosophical basis for my faith, and it would be a system of logic quite as sound as that which anyone could work out against it—more so, I am confident. The logic is convincing to me, but if I had to accept it solely upon cold logic, it would mean little. As James Martineau said, "We do not believe in immortality because we can prove it, but we try to prove it because we cannot help believing it."

Thus it is not my purpose to attempt to prove the thesis of immortality; only to state my faith. I believe in immortality with a strong and steady conviction. I believe that when my loved ones pass into the great beyond, I shall see them again. I believe there is an end of tears.

Only you can convince yourself of immortality, for it is not a demonstration or a proposition. It is, and must forever be, a deep conviction or instinct. "The faith of immortality," says Horace Bushnell, "depends upon a sense of it begotten and not an argument for it concluded."

I can tell you, however, how to deepen your faith. There are two things you must do: the first is to look deeply into the soul of man—not man as he appears to be, but man as he is in his heart; the second is to get near to the heart of God. When one examines the human heart at close range, he becomes aware of a greatness and a fundamental goodness. Superficial observation of man makes apparent his many imperfections, but a deeper study reveals a grandeur which Emmanuel Kant said filled him with constantly increasing admiration and awe, so that he compared the inner worth of man to the glory of the starry heavens.

Surely, also, no writer ever knew men with such sure instinct as did Shakespeare. The Bard of Avon is the supreme literary genius of the world because of his uncanny knowledge of man. He says, "What a piece of work is man! how noble in reason! how infinite in faculty! in form and moving how express and admirable! in action how like an angel! in apprehension how like a god; the beauty of the world! the paragon of animals!"

Looking into man in this manner we shall surely find ourselves in agreement with John Oxenham:

> *In every soul of all mankind*
> *Somewhat of Christ I find,*
> *Somewhat of Christ—and thee;*
> *For in each one there surely dwells*
> *That something which most surely spells*
> *Life's immortality.*

The second way to get the feel of immortality in your soul is to get up close against the heart of God. As the stern negatives, heavy doubts, fear of death, fears of losing loved ones come like dismal fog into your soul, get close to God's heart, look up into His face, and you will know.

Long ago, when I was a little fellow, with my father and mother I was on the old Ohio riverboat *The Island Queen*, coming at night into her dock. It was a stormy night and some confusion had arisen in warping the boat into her pier, which sent a near panic through the people. The tense atmosphere, the storm clouds, the lightning all combined to put fear into the heart of a little boy. I looked over the side of the vessel, down to the dark, swirling waters and was afraid. I can remember even now with healing comfort, snuggling close up against the side of my father and looking up into his face; whereupon he smiled confidently at me and I was no longer afraid. In similar manner, as our little craft makes its way over the stormy sea of life and as we feel the mist in our faces and know we are nearing the place, like Robert Browning in "Paracelsus" one may say:

If I stoop
Into a dark tremendous sea of cloud,
It is but for a time; I press God's lamp
Close to my breast; its splendor, soon or late,
Will pierce the gloom; I shall emerge one day.

As the veteran pilot can hear the far-off sound of bells above the storm, which others cannot discern, so he who knows the ways of God and man can catch intimations of eternal coastlines.

Thus he who has looked deeply into the heart of man and God may not, it is true, understand all, but he has caught reflections, foretokens, intimations of immortality. It is unwise, for the reason that it is futile, to approach this matter scientifically. In the first place, it is out of the realm of science; it is a "beyond science" question. It is beyond science because science does and can deal only with the facts of the physical world that can be measured, weighed, accurately observed, and classified. The fact of immortality belongs not to the natural sciences but to philosophy and religion. Moreover, scientific considerations for or against the belief in immortality are practically meaningless. Nor should we give much consideration to scientific disproofs concerning immortality, for usually they are not worth the paper they are written on. The simple fact is that science has no data.

When we approach this question from the purely scientific point of view, the best we can do is to balance one set of evidence against the other and then deduce what we will, which, of course, leads us instantly back into the region of faith. It might be remembered that science itself depends upon intimations, inspirations, even faith, for, as Lord Kelvin told us long ago, when the scientist comes to the end of demonstration, he must take what Kelvin called a mortal leap to come finally to truth. Thus, if in scientific inquiry the gleam of intimations leads the scientist on, so may we in this field have confidence in the validity and accuracy of our intimations of immortality. So, James Russell Lowell, in "The Cathedral," is dealing with sound doctrine when he exclaims, "We sometimes have intimations clear of wider scope, hints of occasions infinite."

The validity of the intimations of immortality is attested by the notable people who have felt them. The finest minds and most sensitive souls among us have followed this instinct of immortality with a childlike faith. John Morley waves a gallant farewell as he concludes his *Book of Recollections*, saying, "So to my home and in the falling twilight." To what home did he refer? Surely no other than that promised by Jesus—"I go to prepare a place for you."

Alfred Tennyson, one of the finest souls of our Anglo-Saxon heritage, calls out in faith:

Thou wilt not leave us in the dust,
Thou madest man, he knows not why;
He thinks he was not made to die.
Thou hast made him; thou art just.

Robert Louis Stevenson, that joyous and eternally youthful spirit, despite his long battle with the medicine bottle, awaits the touch of death in his island in the Pacific with these brave words:

The breeze from the embalmed land
Blows sudden toward the shore
And claps my cottage door—
I hear the signal, Lord,
I understand;
The night at thy command
Comes;
I will eat and sleep,
And will not question more.

Can these fine minds have been wrong? Is it possible that they and countless other, though less famous, men and women have been deluded? Can the lofty intuitions of these sensitive spirits be false? Like Job, who among us has not cried, "If a man die, shall he live again?"

We have considered the arguments for and against; we have weighed the evidence and scanned the horizon of the years and have been unsatisfied. Then, at last, in the regions of faith, ringing clearly like the notes of a silver bell, we have heard a voice vibrant with authority, the voice of Jesus: "If it were *not* so, I would have told you." Thus we may believe that the deepest intuitions and profoundest faith of the human soul in its moments of luminous insight will not betray us. The intimation of immortality finds definite basis in two great facts— what God is and what man is. It finds its validity in the worth of man and the character of God. What values are there in human life that give it the hint of eternity?

There is, first, the thrill of man to beauty that stirs and woos him with an irresistible lure. It makes him conscious of a beauty within.

He looks, for example, upon Mount Shasta on a clear morning, when the great cone of the mountain towers above the wooded hillsides of California, its ermine mantle of snow gleaming like myriads of diamonds in the sunlight, its waterfalls spurting like scintillating jewels into the great dizzy valley, its murmuring rivers wending their way to the sea. He sees and hears and is conscious of the vastness and cleanness of the world. It calls to a greatness and cleanness of his own heart. He stands by the brink of the Grand Canyon in the crisp air of the Arizona uplands and watches the brilliant colors of gold and red and scarlet merging into the eerie shadows until purple twilight softly covers the towers, domes, and minarets of the vast abyss. Standing in the midst of that mighty silence, where nature before his very eyes is carving her story upon the rocks, he feels so deeply that it awes him—a profound affinity between the age-old world and his own soul. He wanders through a woodland, listening to the myriad sounds of life, conscious of the healing touch of nature. He sits beneath a tree and watches the sunlight as it splashes down between the branches onto the dark earth beneath and, like Wordsworth at Tintern Abbey, feels not only a Presence that disturbs him with the joy of elevated thought, but also a something far more deeply interfused that rolls through all things and comes to rest, finally, in his own soul.

Another value in man suggesting immortality is his response to the ideal, to goodness. Phillips Brooks once said a great thing: "We are haunted by the ideal life; it is in our blood and will never be still." Man may fail to follow the ideal life and may not yield to its impulses, but he cannot escape from its constant resurgence in his soul. It will forever lure him. Whence come these mystic impulses toward goodness? Surely from divinity deep within the breast, straining ever toward the pure heights of life. Because it is there and ever persists, may we not conclude that it is ultimate in any characterization we may make of human life?

Man's capacity for insight and intuition also bears witness to his immortality. Intuition may be defined as that knowledge that is above reason. It is man's highest faculty and goes where reason cannot go. It is a quality earlier than the intellectual process and therefore more peremptory and decisive. The validity of the intuitions was recognized by the great thinker Henri Bergson. "Some other faculty," he said, "than the intellect is necessary for the apprehension of reality." Ralph Waldo Emerson likewise supports the right of intuitions to our respect by saying, "When God wants to carry a point with his children, he plants his argument in the instincts."

Once, twice, perhaps three times in a life, under some stress or sorrow, straining our ears, we hear a reassuring voice, and, shading our eyes, we see intimations of an immortality to be. The Christian heart believes that if these intuitions and instincts were not so, He would have told us. We rest our faith in immortality upon the reliability of Jesus. He knew our longings and understood our intuitions. Had there been no objective reality in the direction in which they point, He would have told us. On the contrary, while He did not explain the afterlife, He gave us sublime hope by telling us our intuitions are trustworthy: "If it were *not so*, I would have told you."

The second great intimation of immortality is found in the character of God. We believe the soul was not made to be destroyed but to live on because of what God apparently is. We believe He is intelligent, and everywhere in the universe are evidences in support of that belief. The mark of intelligence is law and order and perfect precision. Here is a great skyscraper towering fifty, sixty, seventy stories above the street. It is built to the fraction of an inch on law. Would we not be very foolish to say that this great universe, infinitely more intricate and complicated than any man-made structure, came into being without personal intelligence?

Moreover, any person of intelligence will recognize an article of intrinsic worth and become a conservator of values. If a person is wasteful or destructive or even careless, his intellectual capacity is called into question. Thus we sometimes speak contemptuously of a fool and his money as being soon parted. Observe the values God has created. He has made men like Shakespeare, Milton, Aristotle, Socrates, Lincoln, and a host of others less known but whose personalities have been radiant and whose efforts have been creative. Would it be the mark of intelligence to permit the destruction of such marvelous creation at the end of three-score years and ten? Would God do what any intelligent individual would not do? The mere thought is inconceivable. No, Emerson is right, "What is excellent, as God lives, is permanent"—in a house, in a world, or in a life.

We regard God as a Father, loving and just. That is what Jesus said He is, and because of Jesus, with His goodness and sacrificial spirit, His beauty of life, we believe that God is like that. Could a father thrust his children away? But one may raise the question: Behold the pain and sorrow in the world. Would God, as a Father, permit His children to suffer in this manner? I think of my own father. He loved me; he would have given his life for me; he sacrificed many things for me, but I remember a room where my father and I used to retire on occasion, where he practiced the laying on of hands in an unecclesiastical manner, finishing with that ancient parental excuse, that it hurt him more than it did me. I needed such parental discipline, else I would grow to manhood soft and with only a partial appreciation of life's disciplinary values. But I remember other times, many of them, when my father in love and tenderness put his hand upon my head or his arms of protection about me.

Thus, when one becomes a man, he is but a child grown larger, and when the Great Father of the universe disciplines him, surely he will not conclude that love does not exist. The assured love of God leads us back finally to that great text with which we may reassure ourselves regarding personal immortality: "If it were *not* so, I would have told you."

So I am asking you to follow no intricate and reasoned argument but to have faith—a faith like that of a little child who believes that nothing is too good to be true. John Greenleaf Whittier gave expression to this faith.

O love will dream and faith will trust,
Since he who knows our needs is just,
That somehow, somewhere, meet we must.
Alas for him who never sees
The stars shine through his cypress trees,

Who hopeless lays his dead away,
Nor looks to see the breaking day
Across the mournful marbles play;
Who hath not learned in hours of faith
This truth, to sense and flesh unknown—
That life is ever Lord of Death
And love can never lose its own.

Remember those words from the Bible: "If it were *not* so, I would have told you." That is to say, trust that instinct in your heart that tells you that somewhere, somehow, you will meet your loved ones again in a land that is fairer than day, where there is neither sorrow nor suffering, where "God shall wipe away all tears from their eyes."

T W O

GREATER GLORIES
OPEN UP

*T*he most fascinating thing about us is our power to be fascinated." This penetrating observation about human nature was made by the famous psychiatrist Sigmund Freud. Even in this sophisticated and blasé age, men still have the capacity to be fascinated. Our latest demonstration of fascination is that of outer space, which continues to hold mankind spellbound.

But the thing that Freud was referring to, and which is fundamental, is the ability of mankind to be fascinated by inner space, by that vast area within man himself where he comes upon God and Christ and immortality; where he stands spellbound, if you will, before the mysteries of life and death.

A long time ago there passed from the American scene one of the greatest industrialists of all time, a great Christian gentleman, Alfred P. Sloan, Jr., builder of the General Motors Corporation. A few years before his passing, his wife, whom he idolized, had died, and Mr. Sloan was inconsolable. I had known him slightly, and he asked if I would come to see him. I went to the Fifth Avenue apartment of this remarkable man and was ushered into his living room. There he was, his face like a granite cliff, strong, rugged. I knew he had put together one of the giant industries of this country and that his was one of the most brilliant organizational and scientific minds of our country. It was said that Mr. Sloan had based his life on the following principles: "Get the facts. Recognize the equities of all concerned. Realize the necessity of doing a better job every day. Keep an open mind and work hard. The last is most important of all. There is no shortcut."

He fixed his piercing eyes on me and opened the conversation by saying, "I want to ask you a question and I want a straight answer. I don't want any equivocation. And I want the answer to be yes or no, based on facts."

"I will answer your question, Mr. Sloan, if I know the answer," I replied.

"My dear wife has died. She meant everything to me." (And, incidentally, it is curious how such a strong man, such a dominant character, could be like a child, dependent upon his wife. It was revealing, touching, human.) He said, "She meant everything to me. What I want you to tell me is this: Will I see her again?"

I looked straight at him and said, "The answer is yes."

"I knew you'd say yes," he said. "I, too, believe it is yes." Then he sat there and talked to me. I can tell this now, for he has gone on to the heavenly kingdom. He talked about what Christ meant to him. I remember his saying, "Jesus Christ always fascinated me. There has never been anybody like Him."

Then, take my Uncle Will. I always loved my Uncle Will. He was an oil man in Texas and did very well with it, too. He was a man's man, a tough character, and had a heart as big as all outdoors. He was the only member of the Peale family who didn't try to act religious. He was religious, but he didn't act that way. My Uncle Will died in New York some years ago of cancer of the larynx. He had had a magnificent voice in his time. I once heard him speak without a microphone to forty thousand people. And they heard him in the last row, outdoors. A tremendous voice. But now they were going to take out his larynx. I would never hear his natural voice again. I stood by his bed and said, "Uncle Will, I want you to know that I couldn't admire any human being more than I do you. You're a man."

He looked up at me and asked, "Isn't that what we're supposed to be?"

"But you've got strength," I said. "Where do you get it?"

"Norman, I get it from the God you've been talking about all these years."

"You mean God is near to you?"

"I couldn't go through this unless He was." Then he continued, "I want you to pray with me. I don't want any of these newfangled prayers, with a lot of stilted words in them. I want you to talk to Jesus right now like Grandma used to do." His mother, my grandmother, was an old-fashioned, a very old-fashioned, religious woman. "Can you talk to Jesus now," he asked, "the way she would talk?"

"I'll try," I said. I put my hand on his head and I prayed to Jesus as Grandma would have prayed. And I looked down at him. He wasn't the kind of man you ever got very sentimental with. But he looked up at me with a glorious smile on his face. I leaned down and kissed him on the cheek. I would never have thought of doing such a thing at any other time. He looked up at me and said, "I'll make it all right—because

God is with me." You see, my Uncle Will was fascinated by Jesus, and he knew God.

Maybe even the people who said God is dead said it out of an indescribable fascination. They can't get away from Him. They have lost Him, but they are still reaching for Him, for they, too, have the power to be fascinated.

I often think of the poem by Francis Thompson called "The Hound of Heaven."

> *I fled Him, down the nights and down the days;*
> *I fled Him, down the arches of the years;*
> *I fled Him, down the labyrinthine ways*
> *Of my own mind; and in the mist of tears*
> *I hid from Him, and under running laughter.*
> *Up vistaed hopes, I sped;*
> *And shot, precipitated,*
> *A down Titanic glooms of chasmed fears,*
> *From those strong Feet that followed, followed after.*
> *But with unhurrying chase,*
> *And unperturbed pace,*
> *Deliberate speed, majestic instancy,*
> *They beat—and a Voice beat*
> *More instant than the Feet—*
> *"All things betray thee, who betrayest Me."*

Men are fascinated by Him because He is the essence of life itself. And when we lose Him we are lost indeed.

Jesus said, "Because I live, ye shall live also." We sometimes separate time and eternity, as though they are two different segments. But we are in eternity now; so if we have life now, we have eternal life.

A friend of mine died some time ago. His name was Kobayashi. He was Japanese and one of the most lovable human beings I ever knew in all my life. His wife sent me a cable, "Kobay has gone home to glory." And I sent her a cable telling her how I loved Kobay. He was a manufacturer of textiles, educated in the United States, spoke good English. He was international vice president of the Rotary Clubs of the world—the first Oriental, following World War II, to be so honored.

I was in Japan shortly after the war closed. During my stay there my wife, Ruth, and Kobayashi's wife, Chizu, and he and I went together to a most glorious place called Miyanoshita, the hot springs of Japan. We spent several days there. One night, in the hotel dining hall, I was about to sign my check for dinner. The rooms in the hotel didn't have numbers but were named after flowers. The room I occupied was the chrysanthemum room and I wanted to write "chrysanthemum room" on the bill. But I didn't know how to spell it. I asked, "Kobay, how do you spell chrysanthemum?"

"I don't know," he answered. "Why don't you use the Japanese word?"

"What is it?"

"Kiku, k-i-k-u."

I liked that much better and signed my checks that way all through our stay. We were having a glorious time together. That night in the dining hall, with a full moon shining over the hills, we got to talking very deeply. Presently I said to them, "You had another boy, didn't you?"

"Yes. He died in the Philippines."

My wife and I had come from the Philippines, where we had seen the beautiful American cemetery, with Old Glory flying over the honored dead. "Where is your boy buried today, Kobay?" I asked.

"We don't know," he replied. "A nameless grave, we expect, for he was fighting your people."

"I know."

"He was a Christian boy," said Kobay. "He didn't want to go and fight. But his emperor commanded him to go. He was patriotic and he went, just as every patriotic American boy did."

"The night before he went," Chizu said, "I gave him a little Bible. I said, 'Honey, take Jesus with you.' And he said, 'Mother, I wouldn't go without Jesus.' Ah," she continued, "I know he was shot along a road and fell into a ditch. That Bible was in his pocket and he died in Jesus."

I put my hand over on Chizu's hand and Kobay put his hand on mine. Ruth put her hand on top of Kobay's hand. And we sat there, late enemies, brothers in Christ, in a sense of dedication and fellowship that was deeply felt. I salute the memory of Kobay, a glorious Christian of another race, with whom I crossed paths on the bridge of the eternal Christ.

Finally, eternal life has to do with life here. Life in this world is vital and vibrant and creative. Christ comes to give us life, not only eternally, but here and now. "Because I live," He said, "ye shall live also."

The day after one Easter, I was downtown in the financial district with a friend of mine. In an elevator on our way to the street, he said, "I didn't go to church yesterday, Norman."

"Why not?" I asked.

"Well," he continued, "you know my boy died. And I couldn't take it. I went out to the cemetery to be with him." I could see that this man felt sorrow to the very depths of his being.

"I know how you feel, George. But may I just say to you, your boy isn't in that cemetery. Only the mortal remains of your wonderful son are there."

"Where is he then?" he asked.

"He is right here with you now, for you loved him, didn't you? He loved you, and you were both in Christ. He isn't in that cemetery."

We walked several blocks before he could say anything. Then, "Thanks for reminding me of that," was all he said.

When our loved ones leave us, we lay away their physical bodies, no longer needed, like coats that are worn out. But at the time of death, the *person* is released into a heavenly body.

I remember when my dear mother died in a little town in upstate New York. We took her body back to Ohio for burial. On the journey we had to change trains at Buffalo. I was walking down the platform and saw on a truck the shadowy outlines of a box. I walked over, almost fearing to read what was there. It said, "Remains of Anna Peale." That was rather a crude statement, and it might have struck me as repulsive.

But the more I thought about it, the more it carried a glorious message to me: what was in that box was merely a physical form that I loved and my brothers loved and my father loved and many people loved. But my mother herself was not there. And when I walked out of the cemetery at Lynchburg, Ohio, having left her body there, these words from the gospel of Luke rang through my mind: "Why seek ye the living among the dead?"

In this world of mortality comes the glorious message that when mortal life is finished here in Christ, greater glories open up than we ever dreamed of, where there is no emphasis at all on decay and death, but only life and hope.

T H R E E

You Never Die

I usually deal with personal problems affecting people in their daily lives. Now I am going to deal with a very great matter—so great that I approach it with considerable trepidation—the proposition that we can live eternally.

I wonder what your reactions would be if I were to declare that at long last it has been definitely determined that you do not die. Still, we have been declaring this very thing from Christian pulpits for twenty wide centuries. Only recently, an eminent scientist stood on the platform of Town Hall in New York City and stated, "According to the minimum standards of science, we are prepared to declare that the soul theory has been proved." This statement may ultimately be regarded as the greatest scientific declaration of the twentieth century.

When I began preaching in 1921, I felt that I had to defend the Easter message against scientists, for many of them had bowed God out of the universe, claiming that His function had been discharged. But today we ministers are no longer on the defensive. Science and religion have joined forces in defending the Easter message against antiquated thinkers.

There is a deep desire within all of us to believe that at death the soul does not die. The Bible has assured us that this is so, and we of the clergy have held to that conviction with faith throughout the centuries. Now science joins us in this belief. I am convinced that one day they will agree that everything Jesus said is right, that His truth is the beginning and the end of all wisdom.

How did science acquire the new knowledge? Nearly a hundred years ago, a number of eminent scientists, among them A. R. Wallace, who paralleled Darwin's *The Origin of Species*; F. W. H. Myers; the Americans Josiah Royce and William James, began investigations into the nature of the human psyche. Then the science of psychology developed, which by definition means the study of the human soul. At the outset, however, this science dealt only with materialistic factors such as behaviorism. Opposed to the behaviorists were men like James and Royce who incorporated in their studies the entire field of thought.

We welcome the support of spiritual truth by the scientists of our times. But people of other times have known in their deeper experiences about the existence of spiritual elements. If you have read Charles Lindbergh's book, *The Spirit of St. Louis*, you will recall his fight with sleep as he drove his plane through the vast sky distances above the ocean. He struggled with his body and with his mind against the overpowering urge to sleep. And, he says, as he struggled, he became aware of a third part of himself that was indomitable and indestructible. That third part hovered over his mind and body, guarding them, strengthening them. It is that third element that science now claims to have proven indestructible. That is the immortal soul.

Scientists started their early experiments by investigating the belief that the dead returned to enter into the life-state of the living. The first case of this kind to receive attention in the United States concerned a man named Chaffin, who died in North Carolina in 1921. He had made a will in 1905 leaving his property to his youngest son, Marshall. The family was upset, thinking the estate should have gone to the oldest son,

James. One night the second son, John, had a dream in which his father appeared to him in the same long, black overcoat he had worn for over ten years and which had become inextricably connected with him. In the dream the father opened the coat and pointed to the inside pocket.

John awakened in a cold sweat. He remembered that James now had that overcoat. He traveled to James's home, twenty miles distant, and told them his dream. James's wife got the overcoat and, with trembling fingers, John unfolded it to find that the inside pocket was sewn shut. He ripped it open and found in it a piece of paper on which was written, "Read the twenty-seventh chapter of Genesis in my daddy's old Bible."

Their grandfather, the daddy of the note, had been a preacher. His Bible was in another county. Both sons went there and examined the Bible. Between the pages of the specified chapter in Genesis they found a later will bequeathing the estate to all the children. They took this will to court. Under the law of North Carolina, a will did not have to be attested so long as it was in the handwriting of the deceased, and everybody admitted that this was in the father's handwriting. The first will was set aside and the second admitted to probate.

Such stories are not meant to sound like amusing experiences. Dealing with faculties of the human mind is a serious matter. The churches have always said the soul lives, but they have not been able to scientifically demonstrate that fact. They believe it on the authority of Jesus Christ, the historical Jesus, who was seen by many at His physical death. He was seen by many on His reappearances after that death. By these events Jesus was showing us that this element we call the soul is indestructible.

A girl dying of tuberculosis (this is a well-authenticated case) was in a state of unconsciousness. She was heard to call out, "I see Susan, Ellie, Barry!" These were her three sisters, all of whom had been gone from this world for some time. Then she said, " I see Edward; I didn't know Edward was there!"

Neither did anyone else in the family. But three weeks after this girl had died, they received a letter from a foreign country where he had been living; Edward had passed from this world two weeks before his sister.

Many people, as they enter death, have told us that what they "see" is beautiful; and they often speak of "seeing" loved ones. Christians have long accepted this as true. And now science itself makes it clear that anyone who does not believe in the immortality, the deathlessness, of the soul is antiquated in his thinking.

Jesus Christ said this twenty centuries ago. And the sooner the world comes to believe that everything else He said is also true—that the wisest, subtlest mind that ever lived was in Jesus Christ—the better it will be for the world. Any of us who has had to say good-bye to father or mother, sister, brother, husband, wife, or child has had a heavy heart. That is understandable, for we are human. But our Lord and Savior says they are still with us. Now great scholars also are telling us that they are still with us.

Therefore, the greatest truth ever uttered in the history of the world is being declared by religion, philosophy, and science to be absolutely trustworthy. You can believe it. It is this: "I am the resurrection, and the life: he that believeth in me, though he were dead, yet shall he live: And whosoever liveth and believeth in me shall never die" (John 11:25–26). So be happy; be filled with joy; be glad; live with power; and live as is fitting for those who never die.

F O U R

CITIZENS
OF ETERNITY

*T*he most exciting thing ever to come into this world is the system of thought and action known as the Gospel of Jesus Christ. Now obviously I do not refer to those dull, lifeless, antiquated forms that are sometimes associated, God help us, with Christianity. I refer to that flaming thing that began in Galilee and Judea and, passing like hallowed fire from heart to heart, swept over the ancient world and changed the face of history—that lilting, vital, spiritual thing that nothing can destroy, which is truly the pure Gospel of the Lord Jesus Christ. There has never been anything like it.

Think what it offers—the incredible blessings it gives to human beings! The Bible itself becomes astonished at its promises, for it runs out of words and says, "Eye hath not seen, nor ear heard, neither have entered into the heart of man, the things which God hath prepared for them that love him."

What does the Gospel offer? Courage over fear, for one thing; strength over weakness, for another; vitality over sickness; love over hate. One thing after another! The most desirable blessings known on this earth—what a Gospel! How exciting it is! And the climax is that it makes us the incredible offer of eternal life over death. It tells us that we are citizens of eternity. Furthermore, it tells us that eternity is not some time slot far out in the future after we have died on this earth; it tells us that we are in eternity now. Man takes the constant flow of time and puts little divisions and barriers up and calls them years, decades, centuries, eons; but there are no divisions in God's everlasting flow of time. You are eternal now.

The Scriptures also tell us how the amazing eternal life that God offers us is obtained. It's very simple: "He that hath the Son hath life. . . ." If you have Jesus Christ in your heart, you are eternally alive. "And this is life eternal, that they might know thee the only true God, and Jesus Christ, whom thou hast sent." And that majestic statement: "I am the resurrection, and the life: he that believeth in me, though he were dead, yet shall he live: And whosoever liveth and believeth in me shall never die." I tell you, that is the greatest message that has ever been uttered in all the history of man. Through Christ, you can enter into a life that is victorious over death itself.

Fortunately, there are some people who do more than just listen to these words. They accept this offer. One of them was Eli J. Perry of Perry, Perry, and Perry—lawyers of Kinston, North Carolina—a dear friend of mine. This man was a great scholar, a graduate with honors of the University of North Carolina and of Harvard Law School. He was a distinguished member of the North Carolina bar. He was an active citizen in his community—highly respected for a balanced, keen mind. He had the finest religious library I've ever seen in a private home, and he conditioned himself across the years to know Jesus Christ. He really knew Him too. That is very evident from a letter his son Dan wrote to me telling of his father's death:

My father experienced the transition yesterday. He looked at this transition as being a wonderful and glorious event. He told us several times after learning from the doctors of his serious condition, "Boys, I am about to have the greatest experience a man can have, either way it turns out. If God sees fit to heal me, I will be in a position to be a great witness to Christ, having gone down in the valley and then back up again. On the other hand, if God calls me home, I will have the greatest experience in life. And so I will win, either way you look at it."

Well, on the day he died, Eli Perry dictated five letters. One was to me. Here is what it says:

Dear Norman:

This is one letter I hate to write to you, and yet it is a joyous letter. About two months ago, the doctors analyzed my condition as a malignant lung, and I've been in the hospital taking cobalt treatments.

But life becomes more wonderful every day I live. It is joyous irrespective of the discomfort and pain that are in my body, knowing that I am one with God. I know that He is my Father, and I know that life is eternal and that the Spirit of God dwells in me. I am immortal. I am living in immortality now and always will be. You know, Jesus is the greatest individual who ever lived. I learn this more every day. Bless His Holy Name. I talk to Him and talk to Him and He is just wonderful. I know whereof I speak. Christ is the answer to all our problems. How glorious that is!

God bless you and Ruth. I always loved you both. I hoped that I could spend some time with you again, but that is life. Anyway, I don't have to be with you, my friends, physically, for I am with you in consciousness. I am immortal.

Eli Perry is an example of a kind of human being Jesus Christ produces—the ones who listen to the Gospel, believe it, and accept exciting eternal life!

Now why is this exciting message believable? One reason is that it is intellectually reasonable and demonstrable to believe that the human being is immortal. My good friend the late Don Belding was a great businessman and a deep thinker, as well. He, too, struggled with cancer. He wrote his thoughts to me as he undertook to prove our immortality. As has been said, we don't believe in immortality because we can prove it, but we try to prove it because we can't help believing in it. That is what Don Belding did. And he based his reasoning on several laws.

One such law is the law of opposites, which is the balance wheel of universal order. There is high and there is low, warm and cold, wet and dry, night and day, sunset and sunrise. There is material; therefore, in the very nature of things, there has to be spiritual. If man is material, he is also, by the application of scientific creation, spiritual.

There is the law of duplication. In all human beings there is the reproduction of physical characteristics. A son looks like his father. A daughter looks like her mother. There is the gentleness in the voice. There is the same carriage and bearing.

Then there is the law of transformation. We might take one of the pews from the church and burn it up. Would we have destroyed it? The pew as such, yes; but not its substance: the fire merely transforms the wood into other forms. Nothing material is ever destroyed. Now what kind of a Creator would He be who would ordain such indestructibility for material things but not for spiritual things? The logic is irrefutable, as I see it.

Then there is the law of adaptation. If you will feel your ears, you will find little points on the top which come down from your ancestors. Man used to have a flexible ear that could move in several directions in order to detect an enemy. Some scientists predict that if man continues for another fifty years to drive automobiles that require stepping on a gas pedal, he will develop a new muscle across the instep of his foot to give it more strength, reduce tension, and make for greater flexibility. The human body adapts. Now, reasons Mr. Belding, since man has a longing to be reunited with his departed loved ones (a universal longing), surely his soul will by adaptation achieve the immortality which it desires. Immortality is a rational assumption.

For generations now men have been scientifically exploring the material aspects of the universe, and as a result we have developed the greatest material civilization in the history of mankind. Until much more recently, however, there was hardly any systematic scientific inquiry into man's spiritual experiences.

There are powerful forces in the human mind that transcend materiality. You have no idea of how wonderful you really are. You have a soul that inhabits a body, but only for a time. Thereafter, it will live forever on its own.

If God can do what He does with human beings here on earth, He surely can do wonderful things with them in the afterlife. Resurrection doesn't occur only after you die. It occurs now, in the present flow of eternity. I have met resurrected people. There are resurrected people reading this now.

A very dear friend of mine by the name of Paul Soupiset passed away. He lived in San Antonio, Texas. He was a businessman—ran a store—but beyond that he was a servant of God. He got hold of a little, unused church in the center of San Antonio in the square called La Villita, and every Sunday afternoon he would hold services there. He was made a local preacher by his denomination. I used to hear from him because he said his life had been changed, praise the Lord, through a television program Mrs. Peale and I conducted some years back. So we were friends.

He wrote me that someone had given him some bells, a carillon, to put in the steeple of his little church, and he wanted me to come down and dedicate these bells, for he was going to name them in my honor. Well, I thought that was worth a trip to San Antonio, and I went. And they had a dedication service for the bells. But the thing that happened afterward was what I'll never forget. Paul Soupiset told the congregation that anybody who wanted his life changed should come up and kneel at the altar. And you never saw anything like it. There were Mexicans, black people, white people, rich people, poor people. I remember there was one white-haired lady, wearing furs and diamond bracelets, kneeling next to a Mexican who looked as though he had come right off a horse. Paul went and put his hand on the head of the white-haired lady. He asked, "Honey, what are you looking for?"

"Ah," she said, "Reverend Soupiset, I'm looking for Jesus. I want my life changed. I am a miserable, sinful old woman."

"My hand is on your head," he said, "and that is the symbol of the hand of Jesus and the power to resurrect you is now pouring into you, honey." She looked up with a beautiful smile on her face.

Then he stood in front of the Mexican and asked, "What do you want, hombre?"

The man answered, "Jesus."

"I put my hand on your head," Paul said, "and the power of the living God is flowing into you to resurrect you."

In the same way, he touched and spoke to each one. I sat there with my eyes blinded by tears. It was all so full of love. Later he said to me, "My friend, if God can resurrect people like this now, I think He can resurrect us after we die, so that we may live an exciting, eternal life." Well, I think so, too.

God does everything right. God has given us a beautiful world, with great hills, blue skies and clean, fresh rivers; and man is destroying it with his dirt and filth. Man must be an awful problem to God. Yet God takes care of him here on earth, watches over him, sustains him, is his friend always until life's evening comes. And do you mean to tell me that God is going to change His nature when you die? That He is going to forget you? He, who has done everything for you, who has poured out His love for you? Is He going to forget you? Not on your life! If He loves you like that here, He'll love you like that over there. Your loved ones who have gone there before you still live. He has taken care of them. He is loving them like He loves you—even more so, for now they are closer to Him.

I read years ago some brief reflections by the author Leslie D. Weatherhead, who preached for many years at City Temple in London, a great preacher and the writer of many books. In the passage I am now recalling, he pictures a little baby lying up under his mother's heart in the prenatal state. This baby has just everything going for him. He is in a nice warm place. The mother, who goes to all kinds of trouble to eat right things and take care of herself, provides all the nourishment he can take. He does nothing but sleep, take it easy, and eat. He is just having the time of his life there under his mother's heart.

Suppose somebody could talk to him and say, "Look, you're not going to stay there. This is only for a short time. You are going to be born." To us it is "born," but to him it would mean, "You are doing to die"—that is, to die out of this place where you are. And he would think, "I don't want to die out of this place. I like it here. I don't want to be *born*."

Nevertheless, the day comes and the miracle of birth takes place, and the next thing he knows he is lying in strong, soft arms. There is a face looking down at him, eyes just brimming over with love; and that strange and wonderful being hugs him up to her breast—on the outside now, not on the inside. And all he has to do is utter a little cry, and everybody runs to his service. After a while he thinks, "Why, this is a great place here. I never had it so good."

Then, later, he is a little child. The whole world is filled with wonder. Everything is exciting. And in time he grows into youth, and he feels the strength of his wings—the strength of his mind and the strength of his heart—and he has the time of his life. Then he comes to strong middle age, where he begins to reap the benefits of his work. And life is good.

Presently the middle years have passed, and he comes to be what people call an old man. One day the thought comes to him, "You're going to die. You're going to leave this world." He thinks, "I don't want to leave here. I love the sun. I love the feel of rain on my face. I love the crunch of snow under my feet. I like the warmth of a wood fire. I love my family and my friends. I don't want to die."

But the day comes when the miracle of death takes place, and he dies out of this world and is born into another one. The minute he does what we call *die*, he does what God calls *being born*. And once again he feels strong, loving arms and sees a wonderful kindly face looking down at him. And gathered around him are loved ones whom he has loved once and lost a while, and everything is so much *more* beautiful, so much *more* wonderful. And he realizes, I have been born again! So now twice he has been through the experience of death and birth.

God's laws are absolutely accurate and unchanging. The buds in the trees come back every spring, as they have done every year you have been alive. God is invariable; He is the same. So you just use your reason, plus your faith, and you'll know that all is well, both on this side of death and on the other side, with you and soul. You are a "citizen of eternity." Thanks be to God.

F I V E

WE ARE NOT ALONE

I made a great mistake in waiting so long in my life before visiting the Holy Land. Anybody who ever intends to be a preacher should go to the Holy Land when he is young, even if he has to get along with one meal a day for a while to save the money. In fact, I wish everybody could someday walk those sacred roads and look upon those everlasting hills where Jesus walked and looked and stood. It does things to you.

I shall never forget the sun-kissed, dew-drenched, peaceful morning when, with about fifty other pilgrims from many different countries, I worshiped in a garden in the Holy City. Directly in front of us was a tomb, hewn out of the rock, which, tradition says, was the tomb belonging to Nicodemus, a member of the Jewish Sanhedrin, in which the body of Jesus of Nazareth rested after the crucifixion. As we sat in our little service of worship, we could see the open tomb with the stone rolled away. (It is a true term, "rolled away," for the stone was round, like a great wheel, and was literally rolled, in a stone groove, to one side, away from the entrance of the tomb.) We sat there in a gentle breeze with the aroma of the many flowers filling the garden. If I were to enumerate the few times I have felt perfect peace on earth, that would be one of them.

The preacher that morning was a tough, rugged, hard-bitten Army chaplain. He was a man of great faith. His language was slightly unecclesiastical, but he loved the Lord Jesus Christ with all his heart, and he believed fully in the Word and in the teaching of the Scriptures. As he developed the theme of the Resurrection, describing those figures in shining white on either side of the open tomb and saying that it was in this very spot where the risen Christ had come forth, I suddenly experienced one of those immortal leaps of faith that is the way you arrive at truth. I was deeply and serenely satisfied that what is said to have taken place on Easter morn actually did. Now, you may say that doesn't prove anything. I am not trying to offer proof. I am simply relating my experience. I witness. I do not argue.

A few days later, we were at Bethany. How lovely Bethany is! If, today, you open your family Bible and it is one that has old prints, look for the picture of Bethany. In actuality, it looks exactly as it does in all the pictures you have ever seen. A hot sun burned down upon us that day. We stood by the tomb where Lazarus is said to have lain dead and from which Jesus summoned him forth to life again. I said to myself that I would like to stand, if possible, on the very spot where Jesus stood. I walked all around, figuring that at some point my feet must touch the exact spot where He stood. Then I took out the Bible, and my wife and I read the words that He spoke that day: "I am the resurrection, and the life: he that believeth in me, though he were dead, yet shall he live: And whosoever liveth and believeth in me shall never die."

All of a sudden I felt my eyes blinded by tears. I felt warmth in my heart and I knew that this was true. I remember saying that I thought this was the greatest statement ever uttered in the history of time. What words have comforted more multitudes across the years, as they look upon death, as they mourn the departure of their loved ones, as they try to penetrate the mysteries of their existence, than these mellifluous and beautiful words of the Savior of men? Where are there more shining and marvelous words than these: "I am the resurrection and the life"?

One meaning of these words is that we are not alone in this universe. This is a devastating universe. It has beauty, but it also has trouble and sorrow. How terrible to think that we would be here alone in it! The Christmas message is that "They shall call his name Emmanuel, which being interpreted is, God with us" (Matt. 1:23). He took human form and went through all the suffering that a human being suffers. Finally He was killed, but He rose again. The simple message of Easter is to tell us that nothing could destroy Him—not hatred, not the machinations of the priests who saw in Him a threat, not the perfidy of an unworthy politician who sent Him to His death, not death itself. Nothing could destroy Him. He lives and He is still here with us. He will guide us through our lifetime, and He will take us to heaven. This is the simple message of Easter.

I suppose there is no book in the history of mankind that has been attacked as the Bible has been. But it has withstood all of the onslaughts of the ages because it is a statement of truth, and truth cannot be destroyed. One of the most tremendous things the Bible tells us is that we are not alone—the risen Christ is with us. In this world, as we, in society, strive toward great good for all mankind, we do not strive as laborers who have no help. For Jesus Christ is our helper. He will see us through. His Presence sustains us in all the vicissitudes of human life. We are not alone.

Over and over again, I find testimony to the truth of this in the enormous amount of mail I have received in response to books, sermons, and columns. In the course of a lifetime, we suffer all manner of anxiety, difficulty, pain, and trouble. But again and again I receive letters where the substance of what a person is saying is this: I had to suffer this, I had to suffer that, I had to go through so much, but Jesus was with me. He helped me; He saw me through. That is the great thing to realize—we are not alone.

Now, there are times when we feel very lonely. There is a cosmic loneliness and, as a person gets a bit older and the years begin to add up, one by one those who have been close to you across the years wave good-bye. They wave good-bye with a cheery smile, and the place that knew them knows them no more. We long for the touch of a vanished hand and the sound of a voice that is still. I remember when I was still just a young boy, older people sometimes used to say to me, "Most of those whom I knew and loved are now over on the other side. I walk almost alone." Of course, a person should not brood that way. He should keep on making new friends and build the circle anew. Yet there is something basic in the nature of things about this loneliness that we feel.

I was born and reared in the southern part of Ohio. Every once in awhile I go back and visit the places where I lived. In my boyhood I frequently went to a little town called Lynchburg. Everybody has his Lynchburg—maybe in Mississippi or in Indiana or, perhaps, in California or in England or somewhere—some little place your family came from. In the old days, half the people in the town of Lynchburg were relatives of mine—first cousins, second cousins, third cousins, kissing cousins—all kinds of cousins. Everywhere there were relatives. My grandparents lived there, too. I used to go to Lynchburg in the springtime and meet my cousins there. Some of them were about my age, some a little older, a few a little younger. We all used to hang around my grandmother's house.

The door of that house had a bell in it that fascinated me. You know how things fascinate children. It was one of those bells you twirl, and it would ring all through the house. We youngsters would take turns seeing who could make it ring the longest. And long after my grandmother died and other people lived in the house, I used to go back and, all by myself, twirl the bell. On one such visit, I said to Mrs. Grace Williams, who then owned the house, "Mrs. Williams, when your time comes to shuffle off this mortal coil, would you will me that bell?"

"Do you want the whole door?" she asked.

"No," I said, "I just want the bell."

Well, Mrs. Williams sent me the bell, and I have it now in my apartment in New York. Sometimes I get it out and twirl the bell, but it isn't the same anymore; it doesn't bring quite the old thrill.

It is like something I read in a New York paper one time. Some man wrote a letter to the editor saying, "I'm an old man, along in my eighties. When I was a boy years ago, there was a peach tree inside a stone wall in Troy, New York. And I used to reach over from the other side of the wall and pick peaches. They were the sweetest peaches," he said, "and I have often wondered what that tree could have been. How can I find that same kind of peach?"

The editor replied with a letter saying something like this: "You will never find that kind of peach again. That peach had the sweetness of youth in it. You had better keep it in memory."

So when I twirl that bell from Lynchburg, it doesn't have the same kind of thrill anymore, for I begin thinking of all the cousins who once twirled it with me, and all but two have now passed on into the other country. And I have a sense of loneliness.

But I am comforted when I think of another experience. If I am in Ohio and anywhere near the town of Sabina, I go to see an old friend of mine. She is a widow by the name of Mrs. Low Morris. She was my mother's dearest friend, and I remember as a little boy how beautiful I thought she was and how I loved the radiance and rippling music of her laugh. Every time I go back into that part of the country, I go to see her in her little old-fashioned house. She has a picture of my mother and one of my father and a picture of my brothers and me and all our families. The last time I saw her, I said something about her living all alone. "Well," she said, "There is no human being here with me, but I'm not alone." And turning her gaze to her husband's picture, she began to sing in a beautiful voice, "In the sweet by and by, we shall meet on that beautiful shore." I joined with her, for I know that song, too. And there are other songs they sang years ago such as, "We Shall Meet beyond the River." Maybe it is a mistake we don't sing those songs anymore. One of the greatest things in human life is this deep, tender, unquestioning faith of Christians across this country and around the world that the Lord Jesus Christ, in whom they put their faith for time and eternity, lives and that they will meet Him and meet their loved ones again beyond the river.

I believe that when we die we are with Christ. I believe we are with Christ right now, this very minute. Even now we are in the stream of eternity and immortality. How can a soul lie moldering in a grave? When the body goes into the grave, you are merely committing to the earth the physical instrument that housed the soul here on earth.

I believe that the good God who made this complicated, utterly mysterious universe has filled it full of life, not death. A very mysterious universe it is. I wrote an article some time ago on the subject of life after death. I never received so much response by mail to any other article I ever wrote, or so many really stirring letters on any other subject. One woman wrote to me describing her experience many years before, when she was very ill, at death's door. She wrote:

> I saw my mother's face, gray and ashen, as she brought more basins. The door of my bedroom was filling up with people. Even grandma had managed to get up the stairs. They were all around my bed.

Suddenly they were all gone, and I was alone. I was passing through a dark corridor, and many happy people were with me—they all seemed happy. I went forward a little until I could see outside. There I saw a beautiful field of great white daisies shining under a radiant sky; and in the field a little girl, so pretty, sitting and picking flowers.

Then, like a curtain dropped against the light, these words came to me: "Mama needs me." I awoke to find my head cradled on my mother's breast. She was softly calling me over and over again, "Honey, come back to us." I became well and shall live now to a great age.

Where had that woman been?

And here I have a letter bearing the signature of a person famous in the United States, one whose name everybody would know were I to mention it. Referring to my article, this person writes:

On many occasions, I heard my grandmother and mother relate the story of the former's twenty-five-year-old son named Elmer.

Elmer had typhoid fever, and in 1900 that was often fatal. A twin sister, Eva, to whom Elmer was devoted, had died the previous year of the same disease. For many days, my uncle Elmer had been in a coma, too weak to move. Suddenly he sat up straight in bed with arms extended to the heavens. His face was radiant with happiness, and he cried out in a firm, clear voice, "Eva!" And then he died.

When I was a boy, I knew James N. Gamble, of Procter and Gamble, maker of Ivory Soap. He was one of the most saintly men I have ever known. Now, many years later, interestingly enough, I receive a letter from a woman who was Mr. Gamble's nurse. It is not about Mr. Gamble, but relates an experience of hers:

> I had been through a crisis, and I had a strong sensation that my father was near me. Nothing like that had happened before, in all the years he had been gone.
>
> Then one day the most startling thing happened. On the dinette table, I have a pretty shaving mug which my father used, alongside another antique piece. I had finished dusting the living room and was going toward the table to dust it when some power beyond me stopped me and held me as if under a spell. I stood there think-

ing, I'm so glad to have that mug, the only thing I have which Papa used. I felt his presence.

Something made me look toward the kitchen door, and there, between the door and me, was a very clear image of my father suspended in space, remaining there for several seconds. It was a full head and shoulders, very real. Papa looked younger than I remembered him, more robust, with no gray hair, a youth again. His abundant black hair, which I always admired, impressed me again.

My father is not dead.

We are surrounded by a great cloud of witnesses. And they touch our lives. I will close with one more letter. This one came from my stepmother. Once my wife and I had a big, heavy, difficult, tough problem, and we tried to solve it by prayer, by putting it in the hands of the Lord, by trying to do the right things about it in the best we knew—the only way to solve any problem. I must explain that my father's name was Clifford. My wife's name is Ruth.

My stepmother, writing to my wife, said:

Last evening I sat praying for you. A thought burst upon me in this form: Ruthie will do all right, don't worry about it.

Now, I never think of you as Ruthie, you know that. Neither does any living person ever call you Ruthie. But Clifford, when he wanted to be affectionate with regard to you, often referred to you, very simply, as Ruthie.

Why should that enter my thinking last evening? Ruthie will do all right. Don't worry about it. Can it be that we have someone over there working with us in our troubles and in our difficulties?

So I share with you my convictions, which I believe very deeply. You have not lost those who are dear to you, nor have they lost you. We are together in a continuous and eternal immortality. We do not wait until we die to be in immortality. The conditions of immortality are built into human life in our very essence. We are not flesh and blood. The body is only a tool that you and I use for a while. When it is no longer useful to us, we leave it. Each of us is a spirit, part of the spiritual life of God. "I know not where His islands lift their fronded palms in air; I only know I cannot drift beyond His love and care."

SIX

THE RESURRECTION AND THE LIFE

*A*s a little boy, I stood by my father's side in a little burial ground in southern Ohio. We were laying in her resting place the mortal remains of my father's mother. I felt sorry for my father that day, for he was losing his mother.

I remember to this day the white-haired country preacher. I recall him looking down into the grave with respect. Then—without a book—lifting his face up until the sunlight fell across it, softly and beautifully those ancient words fell from his lips, "I am the resurrection and the life."

Young though I was, suddenly in my heart, I knew that those words were true. An unshakable conviction was born. The greatness and romance of those words fastened themselves upon my mind.

Many years passed. Again my father and I, each of us grown much older, stood in the same little cemetery. It seemed but as yesterday, and now we had come to bring to her last resting place my beloved mother. Again, I felt much as I had as a little fellow. Over the span of years, it was the same. Another country preacher spoke, and the words that fell from his lips were the same old unchanged words: "I am the resurrection and the life." Once more, I knew deep in my heart that those words were true, that those words have the answer to the basic issues of life and death.

Those words contain the great message that all of us need to keep in mind. That message says three important things. First, "I am the resurrection and the life: he that believeth in me, though he were dead...." There you have it. A man must die. Men are subject to the law of death. We are inclined to forget that, but it is a good thing to remember. You never want to forget that you are mortal. We are likely to become too flippant, too materialistic, too sensual, too fleshy, if we do not remember that.

We Americans have lost something out of our lives and thought of late years. Something our forefathers had, something our fathers possessed. They were always aware of the uncertainty of life. They lived among hills and by streams; they lived with the simple animals of the fields. They saw the processes of life and death, of nature unfolding before their eyes. They saw planting time and harvest. They saw the passing of the seasons. And they were always thoughtful. In the terminology of a brooding sense of the ephemeral, they learned the deeper quality of life and of the eternity that underlies it.

Now we have become the children of cities. We live in the midst of concrete and steel. We are beset on every side with evidences, not of God's creation, but of man's handiwork. And we have become a little smug and sophisticated with it all. We have forgotten our own mortality.

I once read about a great conqueror of ancient time, Philip of Macedonia. He brought under his control all of the Greek states and their subsidiaries. One of the greatest things he did was to father Alexander the Great, who early in life became jealous of his father and wept because his father did not leave more worlds to conquer. But Philip of Macedonia was a thinker who never wanted to forget that even if he was great, he was still a plain human being. So he gave to one of his slaves, a manservant, a peculiar task to perform.

Every morning at sunrise, the slave was expected to come in and waken his master. Philip rose early because he wanted to discipline himself. If they were on campaign, the slave would come into the tent. If they were in the palace, he would come into the chamber of his king, and he would speak to the king. But he did not call him your majesty, my lord, or anything of the sort. He simply called him by his given name, and this is what he said: "Philip of Macedonia, remember that thou must die."

It is a somber way to get up every morning, but such a statement would remind us that we are in a great stream of time. Our puny hands can do nothing to stop its flow; neither can we anchor ourselves to the shore and be free from its powerful tide. We are being carried on a never-ending stream of eternity.

According to a legend, a traveler penetrated an enchanted forest. In a glade, he found a sundial. On the sundial were written these solemnizing words: "Stop traveler and consider. It is later than you think." Man is subject to the law of death and decay. Therefore, one should be doing something about it. That may sound rather scary, but the thinking is psychologically and religiously sound.

But it wouldn't be true to our Christian teachings if we left it there. What is the next element, then? It is this: This flow of mortality, this constant stream of death and decay, was broken—broken and arrested, and a new element introduced. A man appeared who could justifiably say, "I am the resurrection and the life." It is to say, I have come that immortality may be in your life. I have come that you can defeat anything in this life, even death.

The great message, then, is this: *He is here.* Jesus Christ, whom they nailed upon a cross, couldn't be kept there long. He burst the bonds of the tomb. He is here, living right here this very day. He is right with you, the liveliest personality, the most vibrant personality among us.

When I make a statement like that, I recognize that some will think, *How do you know?*

There is the small-fry scientist who chirps, "I will only believe what I can see." Such an attitude is amusing. What about the electron? Did anyone ever see an electron walking down the street? Why, the greatest things in this life are things you cannot see. Did anyone ever see springtime? No. One day, tree branches are dead, and then some sunlight passes across the earth, a magic wand is waved, and here they are—tiny buds and then, green leaves. No one ever saw them before they burst forth.

Jesus Christ tells us that He is here. And you can find out for yourself that He is here. If you will wholeheartedly yield everything in your life to Jesus Christ and seek Him with a whole heart, your heart will be strangely warmed within, and you will live with a mystic presence.

If you will open your mind and let into your mind the consciousness that Jesus Christ is here, you can go out every day and, in the name of Christ, you can defeat anything. Jesus Christ stands here before your closed mind and He knocks, saying, "Let Me in! Let Me in! I'll give you power over fear. Let Me in! I'll give you power over defeat. Let Me in! I'll give you power over frustration. Let Me in! I'll give you power over negations. Let Me in! Let Me in!"

You let Him in, and there will be a warmth in your heart and a new pulsation of power. You will experience what He meant when He said, "I am the resurrection and the life." It is a tremendous thing, this great old story of immortality.

Then there is one final thought. That is, "I am the resurrection and the life: he that believeth in me though he were dead, yet shall he live: And whosoever liveth and believeth in me shall never die." This is the great old message of the Bible— that you are immortal, that is, essentially immortal.

You are basically immortal, but there are some people who so live that instead of being spiritual beings they become animals. Instead of spiritual beings, they become materialistic beings.

There are some people who wouldn't be happy in heaven. If you live a sensual, drunken, licentious life, how could you be happy in heaven? There are some people for whom heaven would be hell. They wouldn't be at home there. But, the glorious fact is, anyone can change. Every human has an immortal base in his or her nature.

There are some great people who live so beautifully that when their lives are brought to a point of sensitivity they make contact with God here, and now they walk as in eternity. Then, when death comes, they merely step across. They are prepared. But even for those who have been weak and done wrong with their lives, this text doesn't say that they shall be excluded. The Bible says, "Whosoever believeth in Me," whosoever by an act of faith puts his life in My hands, has the essence of immortality within him. He lives, we are saved, to use an old phrase, "by faith in Christ."

A friend of mine is a professor of theology in a certain school. He is one of those men who is very happy and likes to joke a great deal. He is serious, all right, but one cannot always be sure of his seriousness. He had a beloved student who was of a similar type. The two of them sparred constantly. Their minds were brilliant, and sparks were emitted when their minds clashed. They were always seeking an advantage by humor, by philosophy, or by the subtleties of argument.

The student took sick, sick unto death, and the professor went to see him. He was told by the doctor that the student had only a day or two to live. The professor knew that this would be his last visit. He had never been really serious with the young man, so he didn't know whether to pray with him, or to talk to him about immortality or his soul. It was difficult trying to decide just what to say to him.

The student was weak, but still they sparred as always. The professor didn't spar very well because his heart was filled with grief, and it showed on his face. The young man quickly sensed the professor's apprehension and dismay, and he was disturbed by it.

Finally, the professor had to leave, so he put his hand on his student's hand and said, "Bob, old boy, I have to be leaving you now." They both knew that it was for the last time.

Bob looked at him. He could tell that was on the professor's mind. But he held out to the last, true to character. He employed a rather slangy device to let the professor know about his faith.

When the professor said, "Bob, old boy, I have to be leaving you," the boy looked up at him, and he dropped the "professor" and called the teacher by his boyhood name. He said, "Good-bye, Bill. Thanks for everything. I'll be seein' you."

That was his way of saying, "I know. I share your faith. I know that my time has come. I know that I must die. But I know that both you and I love Jesus Christ, and we have given our lives to Him and we believe in Him for salvation. Bill, I'll be seein' you."

So let us all live, so live, that when our Lord calls for us, we shall have had the faith that we can say, "Yes, indeed, I'll be seein' you!"

"I am the resurrection and the life." Don't forget it. "He that believeth in me, though he were dead, yet shall he live: And whosoever liveth and believeth in me shall never die. . . ."

SEVEN

BEYOND
THE SHADOWS

*I*t was a long-distance telephone call that spanned nearly half the continent. The voice at one end was feminine, old, and frail. The voice at the other end was masculine, vital, and crisply strong. It was an aged mother and a beyond-middle-age son who were speaking.

Strangely and tenderly and, sometimes, I grant you, exasperatingly, men to mothers are always little boys. The conversation, therefore, was pitched on that level and she talked to him about the simple, humble, endearing things of the family. She was talking from a little Midwestern village, from an old-fashioned home on a tree-lined street. He was in a towering office building in throbbing and surging Manhattan. But it was a communication between two people who loved each other more than life itself.

He knew she wasn't well and he said to her, "Mother, I am flying out tonight, and we will have a good time together. You just get everything ready, and I will be with you tomorrow."

"Ah," she said, "I will have all the things you like to eat. Won't it be nice to have my boy home again." And then her quavering voice came over the wire, "I'll see you in the morning."

When he arrived in the morning, it was to be told that, quietly and peacefully during the night, his beloved mother had gone across to the other side. There she lay. He looked upon her face, upon the lips that would not speak again and remembered that the last words he had heard her say he would never forget: "I'll see you in the morning."

This man is a longtime friend of mine, very businesslike, very matter-of-fact; you might even say he is sophisticated. I asked him what he thought about that "I'll see you in the morning." He looked at me with a face full of surprise. "Why, of course," he said, "I'll see her in the morning."

"How do you know?" I asked.

"Oh," he said, "don't you remember how you and I and our other friends used to go to those little country churches in the long ago?" And I do well remember. I thank the Lord that I had a chance to grow up in little country churches just after the turn of the century. Looking out the windows, you saw no buildings, only fields and hills and woods and the sky.

Those preachers weren't always highly educated men; but they believed everything they said. And furthermore, they had spiritual experience to communicate; they were talking out of lives that knew God through Jesus Christ. My friend continued, "Don't you remember the dear old hymn, 'There's a land that is fairer than day, and by faith we can see it afar'? And the refrain, 'In the sweet by and by we shall meet on that beautiful shore'? Oh yes," he said, "I haven't the slightest doubt at all that I will see her in the morning." And I don't believe you have any doubt either.

When I first began preaching, we had to deal with crass, sophomoric, cocky scientists who had suddenly discovered the amazing things man could do in the universe, and they tended to bow God out, or at least reduce Him. They treated the Bible, at least some did, as old wives' tales. And people who had a fundamental concept of the Word of God were looked upon askance. Thus began a slow but steady abandonment of the precepts of the faith. Science, you see, had to grow up, and it took quite a few years.

I used to think that in a sermon I had to spend half my time defending the faith. I got over that a long while ago and so, as a matter of fact, did science, because science now has reached out in this universe and found more and more that it is a revelation of God rather than a depreciation of Him. It is increasingly apparent that the whole universe is and can be characterized by one word, *life*, but not the word *death*. So the ancient Gospel comes back now with the support of science.

If you are so old-fashioned and outmoded as to want to raise a conflict between science and religion, you really ought to go back to school. Science now shows that in this universe is a vast Mind and a great Spirit. The great men have always held this view. It was only the small fry, the scientific infantile, who said that science and Christianity were incompatible.

I went on some archeological expeditions in the Holy Land with some of the greatest scholars in this whole field. I said to one of them, "Are you trying to prove the Bible?"

"We are pure scientists," he replied. "We are working simply to uncover what is here. We are not digging to prove anything." And then he looked at me and asked, "What is the matter with you? Nobody has to prove the Bible. The Bible has long since proved itself. But I will tell you one thing for sure: Everything we uncover substantiates what the Bible says about the circumstances of the ancient life with which we are working."

So, if the Bible tells you that there is a land beyond, that there is life after death, that there is immortality, you can be sure it is a fact. And the great minds have always known it.

I have been reading recently the life of a man I have admired since I first met him years ago. While, of course, I never met Sir William Osler physically, I have known his mind and heart. Years ago he gave a speech to the students at Yale which has gone down in history as an immortal classic like the Gettysburg address. He has been characterized as the greatest doctor who ever practiced in the United States. Born in Canada, later he taught at Johns Hopkins and finally in England. When he decided to leave the United States, the greatest financiers in the country offered large sums to keep him here. He trained the Mayo brothers. He trained Harvey Cushing, the greatest brain surgeon of our time.

Dr. Osler lost a son in World War I. The best physicians in the American army tried to save the boy, but his wounds were mortal. Sadly, they had to put the body of the beloved son of their dear chief in the earth. This was the beginning of the end for Osler, for the boy was the apple of his eye, the idol of his life, the center of his dreams. Finally, a few years later, he was taken with an illness that he, with his skillful understanding and marvelous diagnostic ability, knew to be a mortal disease. He was observed in his last hours writing something on a little sheet of paper. When he was dead, they had to take the paper from his cold hands, and this is what it said: "And so the voyage is nearly over and the harbor in view. It has been a glorious journey with such good companions along the way. But I go gladly, for my boy will be waiting for me over there."

Now, are you willing to presume that a mind like Sir William Osler's is wrong, especially when his faith is built upon the substantiality of the Word of God and the permanency of Jesus of Nazareth as well as human intellect and spiritual history? Nobody anywhere has yet disproved Jesus. He lives and because He lives, we live also.

So, when you have to come to that sad experience of seeing someone whom you love disappear into the darkness, just listen and you will hear them say, "I'll see you in the morning." And when the time comes that you, too, shall go into that darkness, realize, to your comfort, that darkness is only the prelude to light.

Did you ever observe that there has never been any darkness that hasn't given way to light? Light is the ruler of the day, the sun; light is the answer, not darkness. I was at Mt. Holyoke College visiting my daughter Elizabeth, who was a student there. We were walking around the campus of this lovely New England college and came upon a sundial on which is the following inscription: "To larger sight the rim of shadow is the line of light." We meditated on it and discussed it. There is no name given as to the author, nor any explanation offered. They teach girls to think, so perhaps they want them to think about this, also.

With small sight you see only shadow, but to larger sight, the rim of shadow is the line or beginning of light. Let me illustrate this further. I went out to Idlewild airport one night to take a plane to Paris. We took off quite late due to some mechanical difficulty. In fact, it was one o'clock in the morning. It was a moonless and starless night. There was rain in the air and some mist; it was very, very black and dark. That is really something, isn't it, to get into a mighty ship and zoom through the dark, heading east over the dark ocean. The stewardess came around to pull down the window shades and I said to her, "Please leave mine up; I want to see what I can see."

"It is dark," she said, "Why don't you sleep?" I sat there looking into the darkness and faintly, far in the distance—you see it was then six A.M. in Paris—a very thin line of golden light appeared. Five hundred miles and one hour later, all of a sudden, that line of light burst into the amazing glory of dawn.

That is the way it is. When this final hour comes and the deep darkness is there, remember, just remember the words on the sundial: "To larger sight the rim of shadow is the line of light." "I'll see you in the morning."

Also, this is the truth because of the universe in which we live. This isn't a universe of materiality. Materiality is only a demonstration of spirituality. The fundamental concept of a whole, wide, alive, dynamic universe is full of spirit. A great London physician once told us that there is no tissue in the human body that isn't essentially spirit. Mortal flesh will fall into coldness sometime. But the owner of the body won't. The whole universe is spirit in material form. And you yourselves, haven't you sensed it at times in those deeper moments that come to everybody? What are you anyway? Mortality or spirit? Do I see you? Do you see me? I see your body and you see my body. We are using these bodies as instruments to carry ourselves around for a while. But you and I are spirit and they that are spirit must live by the spirit.

Many have had mystical experiences along this line. I was preaching in Georgia at a Methodist gathering under the leadership of my good friend Bishop Arthur Moore. He had many of the Methodist preachers of Georgia there with their church members. It was a real old-time Methodist gathering. And such preaching! Dr. Charlie Allen of Houston, Texas, a tall, thin, lanky, dyed-in-the-wool southerner was just wonderful and so was Bishop Moore, one of the truly great preachers of our time. I came along with my poor little feeble Yankee talk. And there was lots of singing.

At the end of the final meeting, Bishop Moore asked all the preachers in the congregation to come to the platform and form a choir and sing for the folks. As they came, the congregation was singing that old song: "At the cross, at the cross where I first saw the light, And the burden of my heart rolled away." As these preachers came out from their places, I was sitting on the platform. They all came down the aisles singing that old hymn. Then I saw him. Just as plainly as I see you, I saw my dear old father.

Before he died he had suffered several strokes and could hardly move, and his voice was in a whisper. But down the aisle singing, with a wonderful light on his face, "At the cross, at the cross where I first saw the light . . ." He seemed about forty; he was trim and vital and healthy and handsome and he was smiling at me. When he put up his hand in the old familiar gesture, it was so real that I came up out of my chair. What the people thought, I don't know. But there were only my father and me in that big auditorium. Then I sat down and could see him no more; but the inner feeling of his presence in my heart was indisputable. So I can say to my dear father, "I'll see you in the morning."

Why was Jesus Christ raised from the dead? To prove, to show that nothing can overcome the power of God, nothing, not even death.

What I should like to ask you and ask myself is this: Are you and am I living in the power of this resurrection? Or are we defeated? My simple belief about Christianity is that if you really get it in your heart, it gives you an astonishing power. The trouble is that most of us have only a weak version of it. But get the resurrected kind of faith and you have really got something that can defeat anything.

Let me illustrate that possession of power in those who live in the power of the resurrection. I sat in my study with a little lady. She sat on my couch and her feet didn't even touch the floor. She was dressed in a Chinese costume, but she was British, quite British. She had that wonderful cockney speech which I always liked. One day in London she went to a Salvation Army street meeting and got converted; and, when I say converted, I mean converted. She became a resurrected person. Then she developed an avid interest. The gentleman for whom she worked had a wonderful library on China, and she began reading.

One day her employer came in and found her reading and reproached her. He said, "I hired you to dust and clean, not to read my books. Besides, you didn't ask if you might read my books."

"Ah, sir," she said, "I am so fascinated with China."

"Read the books but not until after you get the housework done," he replied.

Then she received *the call*. She believed that God wanted her to go as a missionary to China. She went to the mission board and, of course, they were all highly intellectual, highly educated ecclesiastics and they gave her an intellectual test, which she couldn't pass. They said no, you do not measure up to our intellectual standards, you can't go. But did that faze her? Not at all. She had received her commission from a higher source than a mission board.

So remarkable was the career of Gladys Aylward that years later a motion picture was made of it called *Inn of the Sixth Happiness*. And it was a fascinating picture. This little Gladys Aylward, sitting in my study, told me about the times she used to preach on the streets in Yangcheng and other cities. The little British cockney girl told the people that no power on earth could overcome the Christian, that God was with him and Jesus Christ was with him and that if he would become a resurrected soul, he could triumph over the world. This went on week after week.

One day the governor called her to come and said, "We have a terrible situation. There is a riot in the prison, where murderers and vicious men are guarded by only twelve soldiers. We can't go in, they will kill us. And one of the worst men in the prison is berserk. He has a huge meat cleaver in his hand and has already killed two men and terrified the others. We want you to go in and take the meat cleaver out of his hands."

"You must be out of your mind, sir," she said.

"I have listened to you in the street telling that your God is always with you, about Daniel in the lion's den, and how Jesus Christ in your heart will protect you."

"Ah, but you misunderstand, sir."

"Oh, you haven't been telling the truth," he replied. "I only know what I heard you say, and I believed you."

She knew then that if she ever wanted to preach again, she would have to go into that prison. She asked the Lord to go with her and she felt strangely peaceful. She stood at the prison door, they unlocked it and quickly shut it, so fearful were they. She found herself in a long, narrow tunnel. At the end she could see men wildly running about, shouting and cursing. She prayed, "Be within me, Jesus."

She walked to the end of the tunnel and saw the mad man, the meat cleaver dripping with blood, chasing a man. Suddenly he was in front of her. They stood facing one another: the little woman and the giant. She looked into his wild and feverish eyes and calmly said, "Give me that weapon." There was a moment of hesitation; then, with utter docility, he handed it to her. "Now," she said, "get in line, all of you men—get back in line." Quietly they lined up.

Addressing them, she said, "What are your complaints? I will tell them to the governor and I assure you in his name that where possible, they will be corrected."

The resurrected life, the resurrection of Jesus Christ is to give us spiritual power for ourselves and all the world, and the power to make a better world in His name. And all who live with Him can be sure of meeting again those whom you love and have lost awhile. You may confidently say to them, "I'll see you in the morning."

EIGHT

No Fear of Life, No Fear of Death

*T*he one thing that you want and the one thing that I want is life; and Christ promises us life, now and for always.

But just what *is* life? Is it merely physical sensation? Is it a routine of daily existence? Is it to function as a human body? Or can we say that life is an intellectual experience in the mind? It is all of these, but it is more. In its higher reaches, life is awareness; it is profound sensitivity; it is, if you please, excitement, enthusiasm, vitality.

The famous philosopher, Lao-tze, said that life is to be in relations; the more points at which you touch daily existence, the more alive you are. Christianity, with its gift of life, is to make us more highly sensitive toward our environment and the world in which we live.

I went into a hotel coffee shop in an Indiana town one dark, gloomy, soggy morning. The restaurant was crowded except for one table for two, and I was seated at this table. Suddenly I noticed a man at the door and was struck by the happiness of his countenance. The hostess brought him over to my table and asked if I minded if he sat with me, and, of course, I welcomed him. We were by the window and you could hear the "plunk" of the rain outside. But he greeted me with the words, "Isn't this a terrific morning!"

"Well, yes, I guess it is; it's raining, though."

"Ah, yes," he continued, "but look at the rain slating through the dark branches of those trees out there; and see the raindrops glistening like diamonds. Isn't it beautiful?" By this time he had me excited about it, too. Then he changed the subject. "You know, there is something exciting about breakfast in a hotel dining room, isn't there? Everybody's getting ready for the day; there is an aroma of food; and look at the steam coming up from that coffee. Isn't that beautiful?"

Well, I am an enthusiastic individual, but I figured this was really putting it on. So I said, "I'm interested in your vibrant attitude. How did you get this way?"

side and the other side. Tennyson said this side is the dull side. When Robert Louis Stevenson came to the point of death, his mind was very clear, and he said to those around him, "If this is death, it is easier than life." That is what people with great insight and awareness and sensitivity say about the afterlife.

I never knew Thomas Alva Edison, though I saw him once. But I did know Mrs. Thomas A. Edison and their son, Governor Charles Edison of New Jersey. I was in the Edison home on several occasions and was privileged to be present when they opened Edison's old desk on the 100th anniversary of his birth. Nothing had been touched since his last day of work. There were notes on future experiments that he had in mind. It has been said that Edison had the greatest brain that ever existed in the United States. He was a genius, a scientific genius. And he was an exact scientist who never said anything that he did not believe.

Mrs. Edison told of the night when Edison was at death's door. Suddenly it was evident that he wanted to say something, and she and the doctor bent down closely over him. The great scientist, with a smile on his face, said: "It is very beautiful over

"Well, sir, I'll tell you. I really love life." Then he con[tin]ued thoughtfully, "Some time ago I was in a serious accid[ent] and, while the doctors were working on me in the hospita[l,] from some great distance I could hear one voice after an[oth]er saying, 'There isn't much chance for this fellow. He's pr[etty] badly banged up. I hope we can save him.' And even in [my] bewildered state I thought, 'Oh, I don't want to die!'

"It was touch and go for days but, by the grace of Go[d, I] got well. And now it is all so different, so acutely wonderf[ul.] It seems like I never really lived before. People are beautif[ul,] the world is beautiful; even simple things are exciting."

What had happened to this man? He had experience[d a] new awareness, a deep sensitivity. A keen delight had been [put] upon this thing called life that we take for granted and tr[eat] as if it were something ordinary. Let's make it exciting! Th[ink] of it, just think of it: We are alive! But are we, really?

Life is for now and forever. The Bible says, "Because I [live] ye shall live also." Life here on this earth is very wonderful; [it] is a glorious world; it is the best world we have ever seen. [Only] God could have made it. But this earthly life isn't anything c[om]pared to what we are going to have. Tennyson, for exam[ple] said: "Death is the bright side of life." Life has two sides[.]

there." This great man always reported exactly what he saw. Are we to believe that, at the last, Edison, who had been dedicated to exactitude, suddenly became a dreamy-eyed poet? Hardly. He reported what he saw: "It is very beautiful over there."

The sensitively aware person discovers this insight to be true. The other world is indeed a mystery. Where is it, and what is it? Is it in some faraway removed heaven, up about the firmament? I doubt it. God works in a practical, scientific manner. Isn't it more likely to believe that this afterlife is superimposed on our own life; that it occupies, so to speak, the same space? We are impinging on another world that we seldom see or feel but with which, at times of sensitivity, there is communication.

Stewart Edward White wrote a great book called *The Unobstructed Universe* in which he has a masterpiece of an illustration. He describes the electric fan in repose; the blades are thick; one cannot see through them. But then the fan is turned on. Its speed of rotation is stepped up to a higher frequency and, lo and behold, you can see through those thick blades very clearly. Isn't it therefore possible that we can plug into a spiritual current, rise to a higher frequency, and, at times of deep sensitivity, have some form of communication with the world on the other side?

Jesus appeared and disappeared and reappeared to His disciples. These comings and goings were designed to show us that He was not dead, but lived! He repeated, "Because I live, ye shall live also."

So, I want to say to you, my friends, that if you feel you have lost a dear one, that isn't so at all. That dear one is over on the other side, and the other side isn't very far from you. Our loved ones have their own lives and are living gloriously in the heavenly realm. But they are not very far away. And sometimes the veil may part for a fraction of a moment. When you and I go over to the other side, we will be with them, forever and always. This is what we mean by life's eternity; it is an awareness, a sensitivity, a perceptiveness.

This is a great theme, a tremendous theme, perhaps too vast for any human being to try to handle other than merely to affirm his own faith based on spiritual experience. But there is another thing about this matter of life, and that is, you need not wait until you die to be resurrected. It is our faith that we shall be resurrected by-and-by, and that is a supreme experience; but we may experience a resurrection here and now. And most of us need to be resurrected. We need to be lifted from our dead selves to the great higher life for which we are destined.

So, our lives move onward down the river of time. All of us are borne on its bosom, carried along implacably, irresistibly across the years.

We do not think of the destiny of our lives very often. Too often we live our days on the surface and give no thought to these deeper facts of existence. But there comes a moment when the passage of time is dramatized, and we become aware that we are but pilgrims, voyagers, passing from the date of our birth to the date of our death, carried along, irresistibly, on the everlasting river of time.

Some time ago I was on an airplane flying into Cincinnati, Ohio, my boyhood home. The plane came in low over the Ohio River to the airport, which is located some twenty miles into Kentucky. Looking down from the left side of the plane, I had a momentary view of a familiar place. Many years ago, when I was a small boy, they used to hold religious camp meetings in that area, one of those old-fashioned summer revival gatherings. My parents always attended and took my brother and me along.

It was on the riverbank at a point where a little wharf projected out into the muddy stream of the beautiful Ohio River. The flow of the current fascinated me as a child. I knew the might and majesty of that river, for it flooded up into nearby cities and towns nearly every spring, sometimes reaching as far up as Fourth Street in Cincinnati. People would go about in rowboats. And, as a lad, I used to go out on the wharf, throw chips into the stream, and watch the swift current, which came around the bend at that point, carry the chips on down toward the Mississippi.

My father, who was always a boy at heart until the day he left this mortal world, would come there with my brothers and me and join us in throwing chips into the stream. But, as a preacher, he always saw a lesson in everything. He could quote Scripture and always found the right passage for every occasion.

He used to point to us and say, "Norman, Robert, Leonard, you see those chips? Well, don't you ever get too set up on yourselves, because the river of time will carry you away just as it does those chips." And he would add, "Remember to serve God and do good while you are still afloat on the river of time."

Well, when my plane passed by this point the other day, I thought of those chips and of my father who has been carried away by that river of time. But has he really? Have your loved ones been taken away from you by the river of time? Not at all. A distinguished governor general of Canada, Lord Tweedsmuir, some years ago said, "Time does not destroy. Time enshrines."

Your loved ones have not been destroyed. They are enshrined in time, in memory, in your own lives, forever. A hymn that my father often quoted gives a message for year's end.

O God, our help in ages past,
Our hope for years to come,
Our shelter from the stormy blast,
And our eternal home.

And so we stand on the bank of the river of time and reflect upon the passage and meaning of the fleeting years that Almighty God has given us. The Bible is a marvelous book, written by people of insight, who saw the glory and the power and the drama of human existence. In the very last book, Revelation, the fifth verse of chapter 21 tells us, "Behold, I make all things new."

That is a succinct statement of what Christianity is all about. It is not a religion of the old, or something that is worn out. Rather it is a religion of newness.

The fundamental message of Christianity was first spoken to a woman by the tomb in these simple words: "Do not be afraid; for He is risen."

What does this mean? It means that he is with us and that He gives us His indomitability. He confers upon us His priceless ability to overcome any defeat. The true Christian, when he finally gets this consciousness into his mind—that he, with Christ, is risen above every defeat—has entered into the true essence of living. This message tells us, "You need not be afraid of anything; not even of life with all its insecurities, its vicissitudes, its conflicts, its uncertainties, or even of death itself. You need have no fear, if you develop within yourself the automatic mechanism of faith to support you in any crisis."

The longer I live, the more I am impressed by the greatness of human beings. I think people are positively wonderful; especially those who have absorbed the resurrection spirit. I was asked to call upon a woman who was very ill in the hospital. Upon entering her room, I asked her how she was. I was startled by the directness of her answer. With a rare and beautiful smile, she said, "Physically, I must admit, I am not well. But spiritually I'm all right; and mentally, also. I may as well tell you that I am going to die physically."

I looked into her eyes and realized that she was a great soul. I did not, therefore, make the superficial protestation that she was not going to die; she was correct. I shall never forget the serenity, the objectivity with which she approached the event that so many hold in terror. She was like a person making ready to go on a long journey, even a beautiful journey. There was no sense of fear, only sublime trust in the Master.

She said, "I wanted to see you, not because I particularly need any comfort, but to urge you to keep on preaching Christ's message of hope and faith, to keep on telling people that if they find Jesus Christ and have a close companionship with Him, He will help them in every way." That lovely smile again crossed her face. "He is so close to me." And she added another sentence that rings like a bell in my mind: "I have no fear of life; I have no fear of death."

That was one of the most impressive human experiences I have ever had. When I rose to go, knowing that I would not see her again, I stood at the foot of the bed and said, "I salute you as a very great lady, one of the greatest I have ever known. You have no fear of life, you have no fear of death. Therefore, you have won the greatest of all possible victories. Wherever you go in the vast reaches of eternity, Jesus Christ will be with you."

This woman was not afraid of life; but so many people are. They are afraid of everything that life can bring them or fail to bring them, of everything life can do to them. They are afraid, for example, of the insecurities of this world. We have a generation that is particularly afraid of insecurity. Many are afraid of sickness. One reads in the newspapers constantly about people who are having heart attacks and developing cancer and other diseases. I do not know why the papers do it, but they talk about these troubles constantly. The newspapers, in this matter, are the greatest scare-sheets that were ever created in the history of mankind.

People are afraid of illness, afraid of the lack of money, afraid of financial situations, afraid they can't quite do their jobs, filled with inferiority and inadequacy. They are afraid, in the midst of life, of all the crises that life brings to us. Life is a terrifying experience to many people.

How can we get to the point where we have no fear of life? Simply get resurrected, get transformed, get converted. Then your spirit is filled with the indomitability of God in the name of Jesus Christ. You get faith so deeply planted within you that when crises hit you, as they sometimes do suddenly, you automatically can look life in the face and not be afraid.

E. C. Edgar, a British journalist, was an insatiable reporter. He had a very serious operation, and for some reason they could not give him a general anesthetic. But he insisted that he did not want a general anesthetic anyway, as he wanted to analyze his experience. They charted his heart action during the operation, and at times it declined alarmingly. He reported afterward that the deeper he sank, the less he wanted to return. There was a moment—and the physician later corroborated the statement—when Edgar decided he did not want to come back; he was going on. What he saw, as he ventured farther and farther across the river, was something so wonderfully beautiful that it lured him indescribably.

Then there was that friend of mine, a weatherman for many years. I was with him when his time came to die. As the mist of the valley came up over him, suddenly he said to his son, who was sitting beside him, "Jim, I see beautiful buildings.

And in one of them there is a light, and the light is for me. It is very, very beautiful." Shortly he was gone. Jim and I are certain it is to a place of peace and beauty.

Jim said to me, "My father would never have reported a fraction of an inch more rainfall than fell. He would never report anything that was not actually a fact. The long habit of years could not change. He was reporting what he saw."

What do the Scriptures say? "Do not be afraid; for He is risen."

Paul believed in the risen Lord. He lived his life, trusting Jesus. He trusted Him in life and death, knowing that he would rise with Him into that land of beauty that is fairer than day. We, the children of Jesus Christ, may live with Him and have no fear of life, and no fear of death.

NINE

THE DEATHLESS PRINCIPLE

*T*he almost incredible truth is that there is a power by which we can overcome every fear, every form of defeat, even the last great experience of mortal life—death itself.

If I were to choose one sentence to express this tremendous truth, it would be this: "I am the resurrection, and the life: he that believeth in me, though he were dead, yet shall he live: And whosoever liveth and believeth in me shall never die." This, I recognize, is a tremendous assumption, and an equally tremendous assertion. But one thing you will discover about Christianity is that it deals only in superlatives. The Bible promises the most astonishing things, and it can make good on every promise. Even the Bible sometimes runs out of descriptive words, so great are the wonders with which it deals. For finally it says: "Eye hath not seen, nor ear heard, neither have entered into the heart of man, [that is, to imagine] the things which God hath prepared for them that love him."

Usually we assume that the word "resurrection" has to do with life after death in eternity. But in the Bible there is no such time separation; we are in eternity now. We are in the constant flow of immortal life. As a matter of fact, the Bible does not even recognize death as a possibility, except the death of the soul. Therefore, the word "resurrection" means that a man, dead even while he lives, can be resurrected. You know as well as I that there are a lot of unburied dead people walking around the world today.

What is it to be alive? A man who touches life, say, at a hundred points is twice as much alive as a man who touches it at only fifty points. When you lose your eagerness; when you lose your sense of wonder; when you lose your ability to be deeply moved; when you never weep for any cause; when you no longer thrill to the good, the magnificent; when you no longer dream dreams nor see visions; when life has become dull, dead, inert; though you may be but twenty years old and physically healthy, something in you has died. It needs resurrection.

A piece of writing has been widely quoted. It is one of the most beautiful passages I have read in many a day. It was given in an address by one of our greatest contemporary masters of the English tongue, General Douglas MacArthur. Let me quote it to you:

> Youth is not a time of life—it is a state of mind. It is not a matter of ripe cheeks, red lips and supple knees; it is a temper of the will, a quality of the imagination, a vigor of emotions! It is a freshness of the deep springs of life.
>
> It means a temperamental predominance of courage over timidity, of the appetite for adventure over love of ease.
>
> Nobody grows old by merely living a number of years; people grow old by deserting their ideals. Years wrinkle the skin, but to give up enthusiasm wrinkles the soul. Worry, doubt, self-distrust, fear and despair—these are the long, long years that bow the head and turn the growing spirit back to dust.
>
> Whether seventy, or sixteen, there is in every being's heart the love of wonder, the sweet amazement at the stars and the starlike things and thoughts, the undaunted challenge of events, the unfailing child-like appetite for what next, and the joy and the game of life.

You are as young as your faith, as old as your doubt; as young as your self-confidence, as old as your fear; as young as your hope, as old as your despair.

In the central place of your heart there is a wireless station; so long as it receives messages of beauty, hope, cheer, courage, grandeur and power, so long you are young.

When the wires are all down and all the central place of your heart is covered with snows of pessimism and the ice of cynicism, then you are grown old indeed.

And, may I add, you are dead in your soul. Man was never meant to die; he was meant to live. The great thing Christianity offers is life, vitality, wonderment, enthusiasm, power. And the resurrection of the dead is proceeding every day. I have seen Jesus Christ bring people back from the dead. "He speaks, and, listening to His voice, new life the dead receive." I have seen it with my own eyes. I am filled with an unbounded enthusiasm for the ability of Jesus to bring people back from the dead. I feel myself dying inside at times. Life gets difficult. Life gets worrisome. The pressure is heavy. Anybody can die inwardly. But you need not; for He is here to resurrect you.

If you haven't the zest, the thrill, the eagerness, the indomitable power of life that you had years ago, yield yourself to the touch of the re-creative Jesus and let Him bring it back to you, as He can.

If I felt it necessary, I would try to prove to you that there is no death, but I long ago gave up doing that. We do not have to prove it except to satisfy our own inquiring natures. Now and then a scientist will tell you that when you die, you are dead and that is the end. He says this with an air as if all human wisdom reposed in him. How does he know? Who told him? He knows no more about it than we do. But today scientists are coming close to a belief that the old biblical statements about the immortality of the soul can be verified.

I, a preacher of the Christian religion, tell you that I have no doubt whatsoever of the continuation of life after what we call "death" occurs. Personally, I am absolutely certain of it. I am sure that our loved ones who have preceded us live in an area of life that is greater than any we know now, and indeed they may be very close to us. What is the afterlife? I think the most satisfying conception is that it is a different frequency. That is why now and then you seem to hear, as Robert Ingersoll said, "In the night of Death Hope sees a star and listening

Love can hear the rustling of a wing." These mystic experiences, which come now and then, are due to the closeness with which the afterlife impinges on our own present life.

Among many reasons for my faith, I believe this because I read it in the Bible. The Bible does not tell what is not so. I have been reading the Bible for a long while. It has never failed me yet. I do not understand it altogether, but it is perfectly reliable or it would not stand after two thousand years while all other books pass away. Henri Bergson, the French philosopher, told us that we find truth by perception, by intuition. You reason up to a point; then you make a leap by intuition and "get" the truth in flashing intimation.

When my mother died, physically I missed her, and yet presently I did not miss her because I found that she is with me. She was a great talker, but a significant thing about her was that she said something when she talked. It was hard for her to sit through a solemn assembly, for something always struck her as funny. She continually gave me many fresh and creative ideas. I had a wonderful time with her, for she was a fascinating personality. I used to go home to Ohio occasionally and usually managed to get there for breakfast, for that was one meal my mother believed in. She was of the old-fashioned school of Americans who insisted that breakfast was made for men. At the breakfast table these reunions were a glorious time.

We buried her physical body in a little country cemetery in southern Ohio. My heart was very heavy that day. It was in the summertime, and when autumn came, I wanted to be with my mother again. I was on the train all night and kept telling myself that it would never be as it used to be. I arrived at that little town on a cold, overcast autumn day and walked to the cemetery. The fallen leaves rustled as I walked. I sat by her grave, very lonely, feeling very small and sad.

Then, quite suddenly, the clouds parted and the sun came through and brought out the autumn coloring of the Ohio hills, where I had grown up and where my mother herself had played as a little girl. Sitting there, I seemed to "hear" her voice. It was as if she said, "Why seek ye the living among the dead? I am not here. Do you think I could be held in this dark and dismal place?" Suddenly I was happy inside, and I knew the truth—she was alive. I could have shouted. I was so happy. I got up, put my hand on the tombstone, and saw it for what it was—only a place where lie the mortal remains of a body that was dear, like a coat that had been laid aside when the wearer no longer needed it. I walked out of that place and have been in it only once since.

Yes, there is a mysterious factor in the universe. It is a dynamic universe filled with mystery and beauty.

There is a wonderful book, *A Man Called Peter*, by Catherine Marshall, wife of Peter Marshall, once Chaplain of the United States Senate and one of the greatest preachers this country has produced. He died at the age of forty-six because he took everything he had and poured it into the building of the kingdom of God. He wore himself out and died of a heart attack, which came upon him in the middle of the night. He was taken to the hospital, and his wife did not know that she would never see him alive again. She prayed that he be spared. As she prayed, she says she was enveloped by the most boundless expression of the love of God. She was filled with an indescribable peace. She thought this meant that her husband would live, but at eight o'clock in the morning she was told that he had died.

As she entered the hospital room where his body lay, she "saw" two luminous presences. She wrote that she did not see them with her physical eyes, but with her spiritual eyes; two warm presences, her husband and the Lord. They lingered with her for some time, and she states that it was the most intense experience of her life. When they left her, the glory remained.

This is true to what Jesus taught us by appearings and reappearings. It is as if He were saying to us, "When you do not see Me, that does not mean that I am not there." Those who die in the Lord live with Him, and so they live with us as He does. The human spirit has mystic experiences that verify this truth. The universe is filled with dynamic, mystic, electronic, atomic forces, which we have never comprehended before.

Christianity is something alive. It has tremendous power. It is a deathless life principle. It is the resurrection of life over all defeat, over death itself.

T E N

ETERNITY IS NOW

*I*f people will surrender their lives to Jesus Christ, they will have eternal life. I know it as a fact. For when Easter really happens to you, you enter into one of the most subtle realizations in all the world, namely, that your loved ones who are physically gone from this earth, and you, yourself, are citizens of a dynamic universe, a universe that is not material but spiritual.

Now, the Bible has tried to tell us—and why we have never fully comprehended it I do not know—that at the time of the resurrection, He appeared to many. They would see Him and then He would vanish. The walk to Emmaus is a shining example of that. Two men were walking along, and all of a sudden they were joined by a gifted stranger. Afterward they said, "Did not our heart burn within us, while he talked with us by the way . . . ?" (Luke 24:32). Then, when they turned to speak to Him, He was gone.

These manifestations were made, I believe, in order to emphasize to humans that while He seemed to be gone, He was not gone, that He lives. To make this apparent as a universal experience of mankind Jesus said, "Because I live, ye shall live also" (John 14:19), which is to say that the mere fact that we can no longer see our loved ones in the flesh does not mean at all that they are not alive. They are here and alive in this dynamic, mysterious universe.

I first began to think along this line one day when I received the news that my mother had died. I was in New York City; she died upstate. I came to the Marble Church and sat in the pulpit. Now, why did I do that? Because she had always told me: "Norman, whenever you are in that pulpit I will be with you." So, I came because I wanted to feel her presence. Then I went into my study. On the table lies a Bible; it lay there that morning; it has been lying there ever since. It is old and tattered now. That Bible will lie there as long as I am there, and then I will take it with me wherever I go. I never preach a sermon that I do not, first, put my hands on that Bible. I do that because on that morning as I had my hand on the Bible and stood there looking out toward Fifth Avenue, all of a sudden I felt two cupped hands resting very gently on my head. And I had a feeling of inexpressible joy.

I have always been afflicted with a philosophical, rational, questioning kind of mind. Even then I began to deal with this experience, reasoning that it was a hallucination due to grief. But I did not believe my own attempt to reason it away. "Norman," I said to myself, "why don't you lift your mind to a height of spiritual belief and realize you are in a dynamic universe, that the Bible is right when it says, 'Blessed are the dead which die in the Lord' (Rev. 14:13) and 'Because I live, ye shall live also.'"

You can let your mind go to work on this negatively if you want to. But listen, do we not live in a generation of inexpressible wonders? Did anybody, fifty years ago, dream of what we now know about our material universe? And would you be so skeptical as not to assume the existence of this vast spiritual world now beginning to be known to us? I tell you all around us is a great cloud of those whom we love. If you will be very still and look up like a little child, you will almost feel the touch of your mother's hand upon you. You can see written deep in your heart her face and the light in her eyes and hear her voice. Aren't we all little children, after all? They lived, and they still live forever in this dynamic universe.

But I also say this to myself: I would greatly fear not to live a Christian life because I cannot get from the Bible other than that "The soul that sinneth, it shall die" (Ezekiel 18:4). We are told that the people who have life in eternity are those who have spiritual life in time. Brood carefully on that deep truth if you want to continue in this dynamic universe. The preachers of former days were right when they said that we only live as we overcome sin, because it is sin that destroys us. In the modern vernacular, its payoff is death; in the classical phrase, "For the wages of sin is death" (Romans 6:23).

I believe in victory. I believe that the human being was put here to overcome, to conquer himself, his environment, to make something of himself. I do not hold with those who want human beings to compromise and capitulate. How can a child of God not want to be victorious? Nothing in this world can stand against spirituality. Jesus conquers death; we conquer death through Him.

Consider the cross. Did it ever occur to you that the cross is a plus sign? It is not a minus sign. Does not the Bible say that Christianity itself is a process of addition? "But seek ye first the kingdom of God,"—that is, the Cross—" … and all these things shall be added unto you" (Matthew 6:33). Added, not subtracted.

What does the resurrection of Christ really mean? It means just what I have said. It means there isn't anything in the world that can defeat the spirit of Christ in human life.

Resurrection is not some process by which a body is taken out of a grave, or dust is brought together, that a physical body may live again. Resurrection is where you accept Jesus Christ mentally, become identified with Him, are a part of Him, and He part of you, and through this identification of yourself with the deathless Christ you have life everlasting. Living with Jesus is living in mind. Though your body may be placed in a grave, *you* will never be in a grave, never. How could they put a spirit in a grave?

Here, now, is another great statement of these facts: "And this is life eternal, that they might know thee the only true God, and Jesus Christ, whom thou has sent" (John 17:3). Life eternal is to be identified in your mind, in your personality, with God.

Then here is another text: "For we know that if our earthly house of this tabernacle were dissolved, we have a building of God, a house not made with hands, eternal in the heavens" (2 Corinthians 5:1). Tabernacle. What a splendid word! I have this body for so many years. Why do I have it? That I may inhabit it. Eventually the time comes when my body gets old or feeble or sick, and it dies and I am through with it. It dissolves. But the blessed Gospel tells me I am then given another body. Perhaps that other body already exists within the total nature. Perhaps it is somewhat similar in form to the physical body—that I wouldn't know. But it is fashioned not out of materiality, but out of spirituality. Such is the mysterious way of God.

The day came in my life when I witnessed the burial of the physical body of my dear father. I had known him when he was serene and straight and strong, a wonderful man. Then over the years I had seen his body gradually fail, hampered by stroke after stroke, his hands gnarled and his voice so low you could hardly hear it. Then he lay down one day and the earthly tabernacle breathed its last. When the doctor came from his room, he said, "What a gentleman he was! They don't make many like him. The light of reason was in his eyes until I closed them."

So I took my father's body back to Ohio, accompanied by the family, and I stood in the cemetery to say the last words. I didn't want to, for I was broken up; but I knew he would want me to—that is why I did it. The earthly tabernacle had dissolved. And I read these words: "For we know that if our earthly house of this tabernacle were dissolved, we have a building of God ..."

How endless is God's kindness! Jesus said, "In my Father's house are many mansions: if it were not so, I would have told you." God will not let you down in your highest intimations of truth. Jesus also told us, "I go to prepare a place for you ... that where I am, ye may be also." "Because I live, ye shall live also" (John 14).

Get this idea in your mind, get this faith in your soul, and you will enter into eternal life right now. You are in eternal life now. The idea that eternity is off in the future is mistaken. The great realities of life are not blocked off in time that way. We are even now in the flow of eternity itself. Dostoyevski, the great Russian thinker, said, "We are citizens of eternity."

Are you living and using your mind like a citizen of eternity? Or are you permitting yourself to be a victim of your physical senses? Do you live by how something feels to your sense of touch, how something tastes? Remember that the physical tabernacle will dissolve after a while and you will have no physical touch or taste, for they will die with the body. Then you will be given senses and sensitivities beyond anything of which you have ever dreamed here on earth. So now is the time to cultivate the sense of eternity, the faith of eternity, the foretaste of eternity. This is the relationship of man to the everlasting life.

But how, you still ask, do you know all this? I have said we know it from the Scriptures. But the world around us bears testimony to it also. Did you ever live observantly in this world? Do you know really what it is composed of? Many human beings are like a person who goes to an eye doctor. Their vision is poor because their focus isn't right. They go around as if they were in half-light, seeing things out of focus. Then the eye doctor corrects the vision, and the person begins to see with clarity.

This world has been conceived by some religious people as such a picayune little kind of a world. They have figured out a whole little mechanical system and they think that's it. Why, God who made this world is a tremendous God. There are untold forces that we do not understand. And behind those forces are thousands of other forces we have never even dreamed of. Look at what we know through modern science today, compared to what we knew fifty years ago! But the forces science has discovered were here all the time. We just found them, that's all. The whole universe is full of life. And God who put those phenomena in the world also put immortality in the world.

ELEVEN

LIVING
NOW—AND THEN

The subject of this book is so colossal, and the human mind is so small, that perhaps the most sensible thing is not to attempt to encompass this vast tapestry of truth. Perhaps the best thing to do is merely to fall back on the Scriptures, the wisest body of truth ever handed down to mankind, and the most imperishable. Everything else has its day and passes away except the Scriptures. They live on forever.

You see, the New Testament was written by highly intelligent people. Paul of Tarsus was one of the most brilliant men of the ancient world. In fact, scholars have said that he is one of the greatest intellects of all time. And nobody ever took him for a hysterical personality.

When Paul wrote something, he wrote the facts. The other writer who worked along with him was a man named

Luke, and he was a physician. In every community of the ancient world, the most highly educated man was the physician. John, another disciple, was also gifted. These men—John, Luke, and Paul—had a marvelous dexterity in writing. They had the gift of being able to write the greatest truth in the most succinct manner. Nothing like it, before or since, ever appeared in the literature of the world. These men are immortal geniuses.

So, in dealing with a great matter, they go about it simply. And here is what they say: A man named Jesus Christ, the Son of God, was crucified on a cross until He was dead. His body was removed and laid in a tomb. After three days, He, Jesus, arose from the dead. And, as proof of this, He appeared to many people in varying circumstances over a period of six weeks.

Once He appeared to five hundred people meeting as a body. Now, you can't fool five hundred people when a man appears before them. They saw Him. Many of these people lived on for thirty or forty or fifty years after the event. And Luke and Paul drew upon them as eyewitnesses of the fact that Jesus rose from the dead.

Also, He appeared in rooms where the disciples were gathered, and they were frightened. Jesus said to them, "What is the matter with you? Don't you see me? Do you doubt? Where is your food? Give me some." And they watched Him as He actually ate food.

Now a ghost or an apparition doesn't eat food. But still some of them wondered. So Jesus went the final step: "Touch me, feel me. See the marks in my hands and on my feet. Feel my body." This they did, and all agreed that He was alive.

Hundreds of years later, a great scholar from Oxford by the name of J. B. Phillips translated the New Testament into modern speech. In the course of this undertaking he examined, as no man had ever done before, every document, ancient and modern, bearing upon the resurrection of Jesus Christ from the dead. And Dr. Phillips, one of the most sophisticated modern scholars, said that there is not a shred of doubt but that this is true. It is actually a fact that Jesus Christ rose from the dead. On this has been built the Christian religion. Without this fact it couldn't exist.

The Scriptures go on to say something to you and to me. This same Jesus Christ who rose from the dead said to us, and nothing greater will ever be said by anybody in our lifetime than this: "Because I live, ye shall live also." What do you think about that? That is, as they say in the vernacular, really something.

You can find all of this in Luke's writings, in John's writings, and in Paul's writings. The whole story is there in just a few sections of the New Testament.

One day I went with my father and my brothers, my wife and my brothers' wives to a little town near Cincinnati to inter in the family cemetery plot the body of my beloved mother. She was a great Christian who really loved the Lord. Afterward, we returned to the family home in Canisteo, New York, situated amidst the glorious hills of the southern tier. There we sat together in the house from which we had taken her body.

My father turned to my brother Leonard, who was also a minister. "Read us everything you can find in the New Testament about the resurrection."

Leonard was a good Bible scholar and he read the account from each of the Gospels. My father got so excited that he rose from his chair and began to pace up and down.

"You know something?" he said. "This should be shouted from the housetop: 'Anna Peale is not dead!'"

I'll never forget, as long as I live, how his face glowed; and we burst into tears of joy. We remembered that my mother had read all this to us all our lives. And she believed it when it says, "Because I live, ye shall live also."

Now life actually is two sides of the same coin. There is life over there and there is life over here, and it is all in eternity. Eternity isn't something off in the future. Eternity, if you look it up in the dictionary, means always. So we are now in eternity, the mortal side of eternity. Our loved ones who have passed over are in the immortal side of eternity.

And what may we believe about their state over there? And what will our state over there ultimately be? Again the Scripture tells us, and there is no other literature that is more valid. It says, "I am the resurrection, and the life: he that believeth in me, though he were dead, yet shall he live."

That is a big statement. Our loved ones have not died; the body, which was an instrument used while in mortality, has died. But in immortality, the body, as we know it, is not needed. St. Paul refuses to speculate on the kind of body we will have over there, but the personality will be recognizable and alive. It might even be superimposed, in another dimension, on an existence of which we are now a part, because we sometimes get intimations and revelations of people alive over there.

Two people who were in college with me married after graduation and kept in touch with me through the years. He was an officer in the United States Army in World War I, a great, big, rough, unimaginative kind of fellow. He lived through the war and came home with some distinguished honors. Then came along World War II and their son, an only child and a wonderful boy, went off to war and died.

I went to see them. Sitting in the library of their home, I noticed two pictures on the wall, one, the father, in the uniform of the United States Army in World War I; the other, the son, in the uniform of the same army in World War II. We talked about our longtime friendship, and I tried to comfort them.

Mary, the wife, motherlike, began to reminisce about the son's little boy days. The way she described him was fascinating. What in the world is more absorbing than a little boy? Only one thing, a little girl! Little boys and girls together are wonderful. This mother pictured her son as beautiful: tousled hair, freckled face, beautiful smile. And she said, "He was always whistling. Ever since he was a little boy, he was always whistling. He would come in from school, drop his books, toss his coat on a chair, and throw his cap at the hall tree." And, wistfully, she added, "Nine times out of ten he would hit the hall tree and his cap would stick. Then he would laugh and run upstairs whistling.

"Even as he got older and went off to war, the last thing I remember was his whistling as he put his arms around me and said, 'Now, Mommy, don't you worry, I'll love you always.'"

Then she broke down and said, through her tears, "I'll never hear him whistle again." The three of us fell silent; and then, faintly, I seemed to hear a whistle. And yet I could hardly believe my ears. "You know, just then I thought I heard somebody whistling." The father took his great big fist and rubbed his eyes, dashing away tears. And he said, "I was afraid to admit it, but I heard a whistle, too." Imagination? Fantasy?

What is the deepest thing in this world unless it is spirit? For a period of years each of us has a spirit housed in that temple we call our body. But after a while the body falls away, and the spirit is set free. Almighty God, who makes this tremendous mechanism known as a human being, is not going to be so unimaginative as to destroy it. That would make no sense. So we have the promise: "Because I live, ye shall live also."

Life is a wonderful thing. We all love it: mortal life. As Dr. Arthur Caliandro has said so well, "We should savor every minute of life, for every minute is precious." And really, we have relatively few of those minutes in our lifetime. But we are rewarded by that great promise: "Because I live, ye shall live also." He will take care of us, as He has taken care of our loved ones.

Mrs. Peale and I were visiting in England and went one day to the town of Chester in Cheshire. It is a town with a wall that completely circles the old city. This wall is wide enough for three or four people to walk abreast on it around the whole city. It is also a town with rows of houses and shops that are probably built on top of an old Roman wall. And there is an arcade, like the famous one in Thun in Switzerland.

But it was a cathedral that left an impression on me. It is made out of brown sandstone, very ancient, built about 1000 A.D. This day there was a concert at noon, and Ruth and I entered and sat in a pew. Glorious sunshine was coming through the beautiful stained glass windows and lighting up the old, well-worn stones.

Four elderly people came in. One of the men and one of the women could hardly make it. The other two gently assisted them, even though they appeared to be around the same age. They sat in a pew just one or two ahead of us, very frail, very fragile, very old. Then I noticed that the light coming through the window was falling upon each head like a bene-diction and a glory—four elderly white-haired people in an ancient cathedral.

As we watched, one of the men put out his old, gnarled hand and picked up the little hand of his wife and held it just as he must have done when they were eighteen or nineteen years of age. The cathedral organ reverberated with music and final-ly went into an old hymn:

> *O God! our help in ages past*
> *Our hope for years to come,*
> *Our shelter from the stormy blast,*
> *And our eternal home.*

And as I looked at the four, the realization came that it wouldn't be too long until God would take all of them home. Through the years they must have heard the promise, "Let not your heart be troubled, neither let it be afraid." And again, "In my Father's house are many mansions: if it were not so, I would have told you. I go to prepare a place for you ... that where I am, there ye may be also."

And surely they must have heard many times, "They shall hunger no more, neither thirst any more; neither shall the sun light on them, nor any heat. For the Lamb which is in the midst of the throne shall feed them, and shall lead them unto living fountains of waters: And God shall wipe away all tears from their eyes."

Where do these wonderful words come from? Out of the most reliable Book ever written. It is the Book upon which you have lived since you were a child and on which you will ultimately die and live again.

This argument is not scientific, it is not philosophical, it is not occult. This truth is from the Holy Bible. And I believe it because it has never let me down. "Because I live, ye shall live also." But there is another glorious way to look at this promise: we are on the other side of life now. We must live now. If we don't live now, we won't live then. The resurrection is a "now" thing as well as a "then" thing. We must take this life and make something of it.

TWELVE

"HAVE A NICE FOREVER"

*T*he car ahead of me in traffic had a thought-provoking bumper sticker. It read, "Have a Nice Forever."

This, of course, is precisely what is promised to those who believe in Christ and keep the faith. They are promised a nice forever. For did He not say, "I am the resurrection, and the life: he that believeth in me, though he were dead, yet shall he live: And whosoever liveth and believeth in me shall never die"? God promises a forever; and, more than that, He promises a life that is forever new. And death, as John Milton put it, is "the golden key that opens the palace of eternity."

By what token may we enter into this form of life? First, by a realization that this is a dynamic, alive universe, and the life principle predominates. Life in nature cannot be crushed! The crocuses and the daffodils come back every year, regardless of the weather. They come back because they are in obedience to the life principle. Surely if life in nature goes on, the soul of man goes on too! William Jennings Bryan very aptly put it this way:

> To every created thing God has given a tongue that proclaims a resurrection. If the Father deigns to touch with divine power the cold and pulseless heart of the buried acorn, and make it burst forth from its prison wall, will He leave neglected the soul of man, who is made in the image of his Creator?

> If He gives to the rosebush, whose withered blossoms float upon the breeze, the sweet assurance of another springtime, will He withhold the words of hope from the sons of men, when the frosts of winter come?

> If matter, mute and inanimate, though changed by the force of nature into a multitude of forms, can never die, will the imperial spirit of man suffer annihilation after a brief sojourn, like a royal guest, in this tenement of clay? Rather let us believe that He—who in His apparent prodigality wastes not the raindrop, the blade of grass, or the evening's sighing zephyr, but makes them all

to carry out His eternal plan—has given immortality to the mortal!

Of course nobody really wants to die; the instinct for life preservation is built into every one of us. We cling to life as long as we can. That is the way God ordained it, for, if it were not so, we would give up, perhaps, as some people in aberration have done. But God understands aberration and puts His reliance upon the normality of the human mind. But there is every evidence that this thing we call death is not the end, but merely a transition. "This life of mortal breath," said Longfellow, "is but a suburb of the life elysian, whose portal we call death."

There was a scientific meeting held not long ago in which continuum, or the continuance of life, was recognized as a high scientific principle. And recently I read an interesting panel discussion by five reputable physicians on their experiences with dying people. All five of these doctors subscribed to an absolute belief in life after death.

There was the case, for example, of Mrs. Betty Patterson, a seventy-six-year-old widow, who was very ill and who, according to her physician, did die. "She had a ruptured appendix and her body was full of poison," said the doctor. "Although we managed to revive her, by all medical standards she was dead for a few minutes."

When Mrs. Patterson opened her eyes, the first thing she said was, "Doctor, I will never be afraid of dying again, for I felt myself floating. I was above my body. I could look down and see my body surrounded by the doctors and the nurses. I was attracted by the sounds of beautiful music and lovely scenes which I cannot describe in detail, only the impact there. I wanted to move in the direction of this beauty. I never felt so peaceful in my whole lifetime. I did not seem to be walking; I seemed to be above the ground. But gradually the door closed, and I returned."

The second case was that of a young couple—a young mother, age thirty, mother of two children, and her husband. They were in an automobile on the way to visit friends when their car smashed into a huge trailer truck. The husband was killed instantly and his wife lost a great deal of blood and lay at death's door. She, too, according to her physician, had passed from this world; but she was brought back by the genius of medical science. Her heart had stopped beating and it took a team of experts five minutes to revive her. When the doctor knew that she was alive, the thought crossed his mind, "I must now tell her that her husband is dead," and he shrank from it.

But when she opened her eyes she said to him, "Doctor, you don't need to worry. I know John is dead." She explained that she had seen her husband when she herself had died. "I seemed to float away and suddenly I was on a country lane," she said. "Everything was so beautiful, and there was John coming forward to meet me. He smiled and took me by the hand and we walked a space down the country lane. Then he gently turned me around and told me to go back for a while. I'm not worried about him because I know where he is; I know he is happy, and I know I will see him again."

Another man, named James Lorne, had a fatal heart attack. All his bodily functions were carried on by machines while doctors massaged his heart and tried to revive him. He had not been a very religious man—a skeptic, you might say.

During this experience, he found himself at the end of a long corridor where scenes of ravishing beauty unrolled before him. He said, "I never felt so peaceful in all my life. Then the corridor door closed and I was looking up at my wife and my children, who looked so worried, and I wondered why; then I knew. I had been sent back. It's hard to explain, but something strange and wonderful happened to me. Call it God, call it love; my life has been infinitely richer ever since this experience. Something has changed my life very profoundly."

Now I cite these incidents given to us by reputable, scientific medical men, and I could cite phenomenon after phenomenon in this field. Always there is this rising from the body; always there are strains of beautiful music and ravishing scenes of loveliness; always there is this peace.

Do you think that Almighty God would create a human being, with his sensitivity of mind and spirit, only to let him die and come to an end? Jesus says, "In my Father's house are many mansions. . . . Where I am, there ye may be also." You may be sure that your loved ones who have left you are in His tender, loving care and that you will be there, too, when that time comes.

I was reading a story by Cecil B. DeMille, at one time one of the greatest motion picture geniuses in the United States, a very sensitive, spiritually minded man. He said that one summer day he was in Maine, in a canoe on a lake deep in the woods. He was all alone. He wanted to do some work on a script, so he let the canoe drift idly while he worked. Suddenly happen to you. Life is continually glorious! I have been so excited all my life because I have seen many dead people come alive, one after another. They were dead in their thoughts, they were dead in their hates, they were dead in their sins, they were dead in their defeats, they were all mixed up; and all of a sudden they found Christ, and they came alive. Resurrection does not mean new life only after physical death; resurrection means *now!*

God made this life. And He made the fuller life. It is all part of one. It is woven together in a complete fabric. So if this life is good, that will be good, also. It will have its challenges, just as this life has its troubles. If life doesn't have trouble, it is no good, because trouble makes you grow big. And you cannot grow strong without resistance, sorrow, difficulty, frustration. So, even as you have problems here, you are going to have things over there to make you grow; or else it won't be interesting.

I used to hear people say that the fuller life was going to be so sweet, so nice, so lovely. All you would do all day long is play the harp. Now the Bible doesn't say that. The only harp playing is by four living creatures who guard the throne of God. They play a harp. Nowhere else in the Bible do I find the play-

he discovered that he was in low water, about four inches de
near the shore, and he could plainly see on the lake bottor
number of water beetles. One of them crawled out of the wa
onto the canoe and sank his talons into the woodwork of t
hull and there he died.

Three hours later, still floating in the hot sun, DeMi
observed a wondrous miracle. He suddenly noticed that tl
shell of the water beetle was cracking open. A moist hea
emerged, followed by wings. Finally the winged creature le
the dead body and flew in the air, going farther in one half sec
ond than the water beetle could crawl all day. It was a dra
onfly, its beautiful colors shimmering in the sunlight. Tl
dragonfly flew above the surface of the water, but the wa
beetles down below couldn't see it.

Do you think Almighty God would do that for a wa
beetle and wouldn't do it for you?

There is something in each of us that has meaning. A
when the time of dissolution of the physical body comes,
us think of a crack opening and each of us and our loved o
being released into a beautiful peace and joy. Do not be afr
because you have life that is forever new.

But, friends, the glorious thing about it all is that
don't need to wait until you die to have wonderful th

ing of harps. And that pleases me, because it would turn me off to think that I might have to spend eternity playing a harp!

The important thing the Bible says is that God is there, that Jesus is there. And if God and Jesus are there, heaven is a good place. I think it is all bound together. And many thoughtful scholars are suggesting that the fuller life is all superimposed upon where we are here.

There are two professors who have researched this subject. One is Raymond Moody, Jr., who has written a book called *Life After Life*. He is a professor of psychiatry attached to the University of Virginia hospital. He is also a teacher of philosophy in ethics and logic and in what I had never heard of before, the philosophy of medicine.

Another researcher is Professor of Psychology Kenneth Ring of the University of Connecticut. These men have spent years analyzing what they call near-death experiences and have come up with a general pattern. Over and over again, the person returning from death describes the spirit as leaving the body and even looking down at the body after leaving it. Almost always the spirit moves through a dark tunnel and comes out in glorious light. There is a body, according to these testimonies, a spiritual body that none of them describes exactly. They report being able to see farther than was ever possible on earth. They can hear with a greater intensity, have a sharper awareness, a deeper perception. And none of them want to come back.

This research describes present scientific understanding. But I prefer to turn to Jesus, who said, "In my Father's house are many mansions....I go to prepare a place for you." *Mansions* does not mean "rooms." It means stages of development; as you grow, you struggle, you have the time of your life.

I often think of my brother Bob. We grew up together. He was younger than I. He died at the age of seventy. I was making a talk one morning to the employees at the Foundation for Christian Living in Pawling, New York. There were two walls between myself and the plaza fronting the house where Bob used to live and had his office as a doctor of medicine. All of a sudden I saw him, as real as life. He appeared to be about thirty or thirty-five years of age, and was walking rather rapidly across the plaza.

Bob raised his hand in the old-time gesture of greeting and said to me, "Don't worry about death, Deacon [his nickname for me]. Don't worry about it at all. It's OK." The message meant much to me. I am sure we will find the afterlife indeed to be OK if you and I are OK.

THIRTEEN

ACCEPTING
IMMORTALITY

*T*he greatest message of all is life: vital, energetic, enthusiastic, creative, joyous, exciting life. That is the message of Christianity. That is the message of everlasting truth.

A great many people have a very dull concept of what Christianity really is. Some have used it to lend piousness to their own prejudices, thereby making it something that is not only unattractive but basically false. And such a concept turns a lot of people off.

But the Christianity of Jesus as taught by Matthew, Mark, Luke, John, and Paul is the real thing. And it is *so* wonderful that it is going strong two thousand years after it was first promulgated on the earth.

How exalting, lilting, tremendous it must have been in those early days. Someone in ancient times described Christianity as akin to the song of skylarks and the babbling of brooks. Does the Christianity you know equate with that description? If not, you should get to know it as it really is.

The New Testament, which is the true source of what Christianity is all about, says that life is everlasting, that if you believe in Christ you will not die. You will pass through a transformation from one stage of life into another, but you will live. What a wonderful promise. That is really something! Instead of being complacent and routine, as Christians, we should leap for joy and shout from the housetops that we are not going to die. That the beloved companion who walks beside you is not going to die. That your dear friend, that little child, that loved one will not die. That is what the New Testament says and there has never been any document anywhere that is as valid and credible. You can bank on it for sure.

But it isn't all that easy. Christianity does not make a blanket offer to everyone. According to the New Testament, it is belief in Christ, the acceptance of Him as the Son of God, that guarantees eternal life. You are in eternal life now, for eternal means always, doesn't it? So, eternal life does not begin when you die. It begins when you accept eternal life, which I sincerely hope is now.

Some of the greatest people I have ever known, great, rugged, down-to-earth, honest-to-goodness people, have had the kind of faith that makes immortality. One of them who comes to mind is the late President Dwight D. Eisenhower. I had the privilege of knowing him fairly well. And when one got by the aura of the presidency and saw the man as he really was, Ike was a truly great man. But also he was probably one of the most down-to-earth, truly American presidents we ever had. Possibly Harry Truman should be added to that type of leader. They were real, everyday Americans who happened to ascend to the highest position in the land. These men were Christians, believing Christians.

President Eisenhower told me that he said his prayers every night and every morning, and that the greatest person he ever knew was his mother, who was educated, not in the schools, but in the Bible. And when you get educated in the Bible, you get wisdom. She had wisdom.

Finally, like all mortals, Eisenhower came to his deathbed. Somewhere I read that Billy Graham went to see him, to minister as a pastor. And Billy did that in his own wonderful way. According to the story, finally he said good-bye to the general, walked to the door, had his hand on the doorknob, when the feeble voice of the president said, "Billy, please wait a minute. I know that my end is near. Will an old sinner like me get to heaven where I'll meet my mother again?"

Billy said it was heart touching. He went back and stood looking down at the great old hero and said, "Mr. President, General, Brother Ike, have you accepted Jesus?"

"Oh yes," he replied.

"You know He is the Son of God?"

"I know He is the Son of God," the General repeated.

"You will meet your mother in paradise, where she is waiting for you."

That is basic, rugged, and entirely valid Christian faith in immortality. When you confess your sins and accept Christ, believing upon Him as your Savior, you become eternal in your nature; you are immortal in your soul.

I have an old friend—I say old because his body has been on this earth a long time—who is a great soul. But he hasn't much poetry in his system. He has true sentiment, but keeps it under control. He is a cold scientist. He has seen three or four revolutions in Mexico, crossed the Sahara Desert on the back of a camel, and slept under the desert stars.

He always comes to Marble Collegiate Church when in New York City. A while ago, his family called me, saying that he had had a stroke; his heart action was low, his blood pressure low, and there was no reflex action at all. The doctor didn't give much hope.

So I started praying for him, as did others. Whether or not because of our prayers, his eyes opened. In a few days, his speech returned, his heart action came back to almost normal, his blood pressure rose, his muscles reacted.

He said, "I had a wonderful adventure. I don't know what it was. All of a sudden, I wasn't in my usual haunts. I was in the most attractive place I have ever seen. There was light all around me, such light as I had never seen before. I saw faces, dimly revealed, kindly faces, and I felt peaceful and happy. I felt so good that I said to myself, 'I must be dying; maybe I have died. But if I have died, why have I been afraid of death all my life? This is marvelous!'"

I asked him, "How did you feel about it? Did you want to come back?"

"It didn't make the slightest difference," he replied. "If anything, I would have preferred to go on."

Hallucination? A dream? A vision? I don't think so. I have spent too many years talking to people who have come up to the edge and had a look across.

What's out there? You remember Paul saying that Jesus "hath abolished death and hath brought life and immortality to light through the gospel." Because He lives, we shall live also.

This is the mightiest message ever given.

Benjamin Franklin is credited with having one of the greatest brains ever in the United States. Without him, I wonder if this nation's constitution, which is said to be the most remarkable political document in the history of mankind, would have come into being. He was a very intelligent man.

In a letter he wrote to a lady named Elizabeth Hubbard, dated Philadelphia, February 22, 1756, Franklin discourses on this subject:

Dear Child,

I condole with you, we have lost a most dear and valuable relation, but it is the will of God and Nature that these mortal bodies be laid aside, when the soul is to enter into real life; 'tis rather an embryo state, a preparation for living.

A man is not completely born until he is dead. Why then should we grieve that a new child is born among the immortals? A new member added to their happy society? That bodies should be lent us is a kind and benevolent act of God.

When they become unfit for these purposes and afford us pain instead of pleasure—instead of an aid, become an encumbrance and answer none of the intentions for which they were given—it is equally kind and benevolent that a way is provided by which we may get rid of them. Death is that way.

We ourselves often prudently choose a partial death. In some cases a mangled painful limb, which cannot be restored, is willingly cut off. He who plucks out a tooth, parts with it freely, since the pain goes with it; and thus a person surrenders the whole body, and departs at once, for with it goes all pain and possibilities of pain, all diseases and suffering.

Thus, we are invited abroad on a party of pleasure that is to last forever. Perhaps a loved one has gone before us. We could not all conveniently start together, and why should we be grieved at this, since we are soon to follow, and we know where to find him or her. Adieu.

If I were to look at you, standing with a group of people, I would see in front of me beautiful bodies. But that isn't *you*! I cannot see *you*—except for maybe a flash in your eye, or a smile on your face, or some other look that is a reflection of the real you. We are spirits, immortal spirits living in the midst of time.

So when your body is no more, does that mean that *you* are no more? This simply does not make sense. Therefore, the answer to it all is that because He lives, we shall live also—if we identify ourselves with Him, and live in His life pattern. He is life. We join ourselves with Him, and therefore are in life.

FOURTEEN

WORDS
TO REMEMBER

*N*ot too long ago, a gallant lady went beyond the horizon. Her name was Marian Kay, and she followed quickly after her husband, Gordon. Never shall I forget these two, because of the great faith that was theirs, faith of a quality that deepened all associated with them.

Gordon Kay telephoned me one day. "I want you to heal my wife," he said simply.

"But I am not a healer," I replied. "Only God can heal. But I will try to help her as God may will."

When I went to see her, she told me of the cobalt treatments and said a mark had been put upon her chest and back to indicate where the treatment was to go, if in a strange hospital.

Opening the neck of her dress, she revealed a purple mark. I noted that it was in the form of a cross and remarked upon that fact. "Why, I hadn't realized that!" A wonderful expression of faith crossed her countenance. She, her husband, and I clasped hands to pray. I placed a hand on her back over the cross printed there and committed her to God.

As the months came and went, Gordon, who always asserted stoutly that the Lord had his wife in His hands, passed on of a sudden heart attack. Marian fought a gallant fight to live. One day, when I entered her hospital room, her eyes opened wide. "Our Savior entered with you," she said, in her incisive, always highly intelligent way. Later she stated that He remained constantly, and, on subsequent visits, she said, "Our Savior is here." From then on she talked less of getting well and more about how she loved "her Savior."

When finally the end of the earthly struggle came, she told their dear friend "Pat" Buckley how peaceful she felt with God. The trumpets surely sounded as this strong woman of faith passed over to the other side.

One of the great physicians and surgeons of New York City, my friend the late Dr. William Seaman Bainbridge, practiced medicine there for many years.

When he was dying, my wife, Ruth, and I went to see him. He had meant so much to us and our family. His photograph is on my office wall. As this big man, healer of so many, lay in bed, his wife sitting with him, he said, "I am going to the other side. My Lord is calling me. I am not afraid. I am ready to go."

Mrs. Bainbridge, calling him by the affectionate name she always used, said softly, "Will, when you reach the other side, please wait for me and meet me there."

A smile of assurance crossed his face, and his voice, which had become weakened, once again had the old-time strength. "I'll be there, I'll be there," he declared.

I turned to leave. His hand rose in the old gesture that we knew so well. "Good-bye, dear old friend," he said. "I'll see you over there." It was just as if we were arranging to meet in some agreed-upon rendezvous on earth. But he felt just as certain about a meeting place in Heaven. This man, one of the most respected scientific and medical men of our time, had faith strong and sure, a faith that admitted of no doubt at all.

What I want to stress is that death is not the end of life. The great and subtle thinkers in every generation have been conscious of the intimations of immortality of which sensitive spirits have ever been aware. Their words, as gathered here, will, I hope, bring comfort and assurance to you.

I cannot say, and I will not say
That he is dead. He is just away.

With a cheery smile, and a wave of the hand,
He has wandered into an unknown land.

And left us dreaming how very fair
It needs must be since he lingers there.

And you—O you, who the wildest yearn
For the old-time step and the glad return—

Think of him faring on, as dear
In the love of there as the love of here;

Think of him still as the same, I say;
He is not dead—he is just away!

JAMES WHITCOMB RILEY

Waste no tears over the griefs of yesterday.

EURIPIDES

For this corruptible must put on incorruption, and this
mortal must put on immortality. So when this corruptible shall
have put on incorruption, and this mortal shall have put on
immortality, then shall be brought to pass the saying that is writ-
ten, Death is swallowed up in victory. O death, where is thy sting?
O grave, where is thy victory?

1 CORINTHIANS 15:53–55

"Why should we fear death?" a man once said. "It is life's finest form of adventure." These words were not uttered by some minister of religion standing securely in his pulpit on Easter Day, surrounded by flowers and with joyous anthems sounding in his ears. They were not spoken before an open fire at the close of a delightful evening by some man sitting in the easy comfort of his armchair. They were spoken by Charles Frohman on the deck of the Lusitania just as the great ship settled to her doom. He felt that all earthly hope was gone, and this was his last word to a group of friends who expected to share his fate.

CHARLES REYNOLD BROWN[1]

Joy, shipmate, joy!
(Pleased to my soul at death I cry),
Our life is closed, our life begins,
The long, long anchorage we leave,
The ship is clear at last, she leaps!
She swiftly courses from the shore,
Joy, shipmate, joy!

WALT WHITMAN

---

[1]Reprinted by permission from the book *Living Again* by Char Reynold Brown, published by Harvard University Press.

. . . in Him we live, and move, and have our being.
ACTS 17:28

I feel within me the future life. I am like a forest that has once been razed; the new shoots are stronger and brisker. I shall most certainly rise toward the heavens. The sun's rays bathe my head. The earth gives me its generous sap, but the heavens illuminate me with the reflection of—of worlds unknown. Some say the soul results merely from bodily powers. Why, then, does my soul become brighter when my bodily powers begin to waste away? Winter is above me, but eternal spring is within my heart. I inhale even now the fragrance of lilacs, violets, and roses, just as I did when I was twenty.

The nearer my approach to the end, the plainer is the soul of immortal symphonies of worlds which invite me. It is wonderful yet simple. It is a fairy tale; it is history.

For half a century I have been translating my thoughts into prose and verse; history, philosophy, drama, romance, tradition, satire, ode, and song; all of these have I tried. But I feel that I haven't given utterance to the thousandth part of what lies within me. When I go to the grave I can say as others have said, "My day's work is done." But I cannot say, "My life is done." My day's work will recommence the next morning. The tomb is not a blind

alley; it is a thoroughfare. It closes upon the twilight, but opens upon the dawn.

VICTOR HUGO

I ask no risen dust to teach me immortality;
I am conscious of eternal life.

THEODORE PARKER

Death is not extinguishing the light; it is only putting out the lamp because the Dawn has come.

RABINDRANATH TAGORE

Though my soul may set in darkness, it will rise in perfect life;
I have loved the stars too fondly to be fearful of the night.

ATTRIBUTED TO AN AGED ASTRONOMER

We sometimes congratulate ourselves at the moment of waking from a troubled dream: it may be so at the moment after death.

NATHANIEL HAWTHORNE

Grow old along with me!
The best is yet to be,

The last of life, for which the first was made;
Our times are in his hand who saith,
"A whole I planned,
Youth shows but half; trust God: See all, nor be afraid!"

ROBERT BROWNING

I am the resurrection, and the life: he that believeth in me,
though he were dead, yet shall he live.

JOHN 11:25

They that love beyond the world cannot be separated by it.
Death cannot kill what never dies, nor can spirits ever be divid-
ed that love and live in the same divine principle.

WILLIAM PENN

The embers of the day are red
Beyond the murky hill.
The kitchen smokes; the bed
In the darkling house is spread:
The great sky darkens overhead,
And the great woods are shrill.
So far have I been led,
Lord, by Thy will:
So far have I followed, Lord, and wondered still.
The breeze from the embalmed land

Blows sudden towards the shore,
And claps my cottage door.
I hear the signal, Lord—I understand.
The night at Thy command
Comes. I will eat and sleep and will not question more.

ROBERT LOUIS STEVENSON

I shall not live 'till I see God; and when I have seen Him, I
shall never die.

JOHN DONNE

Because I live, ye shall live also.

JOHN 14:19

She has only gone on a little ahead
To fashion a home for me.
There will be curtains blowing,
And books, as there used to be;
Pictures, a desk, and tables, fair
Where friends shall love to come. . . .
She has only gone on as a mother would
To find me a new home.
She has only gone on as others have
Who vanished from our sight,

Others whose lives with ours were wed
Till that mysterious flight.
None shall declare her death to me,
My loneliness deplore—
Oh, it is like her to go ahead
To open the new door.
She has only gone on a little ahead
To find me the loveliest place;
There will be golden roses there
Abloom in an azure space;
Poppies, pansies, and daffodils
And moss I shall love to tread—
O mother! Now it is clear to me,
You've only gone on ahead.

ANGELA MORGAN[2]

Many a life has been inured by the constant expectation of
death. It is life we have to do with, not death. The best prepara-
tion for the night is to work diligently while the day lasts. The
best preparation for death is life.

GEORGE MACDONALD

---

[2]Reprinted by permission from *Creator Man* by Angela Morgan, published by Dodd, Mead & Company, Inc.

Spend your brief moment according to nature's law, and serenely greet the journey's end as an olive falls when it is ripe, blessing the branch that bare it, and giving thanks to the tree that gave it life.

MARCUS AURELIUS

In the bottom of an old pond lived some grubs who could not understand why none of their groups ever came back after crawling up the stems of the lilies to the top of the water. They promised each other that the next one who was called to make the upward climb would return and tell what happened to him. Soon one of them felt an urgent impulse to seek the surface; he rested himself on the top of a lily pad and went through a glorious transformation which made him a dragonfly with beautiful wings. In vain he tried to keep his promise. Flying back and forth over the pond, he peered down at his friends below. Then he realized that even if they could see him they would not recognize such a radiant creature as one of their number.

The fact that we cannot see our friends or communicate with them after the transformation, which we call death, is no proof that they cease to exist.

WALTER DUDLEY CAVERT[3]

---

[3]Reprinted by permission.

For we know that if our earthly house of this tabernacle were dissolved, we have a building of God, an house not made with hands, eternal in the heavens.

2 CORINTHIANS 5:1

A good man never dies—
In worthy deed and prayer
And helpful hands, and honest eyes,
If smiles or tears be there;
Who lives for you and me—
Lives for the world he tries
To help—he lives eternally.
A good man never dies.

Who lives to bravely take
His share of toil and stress
And, for his weaker fellows' sake,
Makes every burden less—
He may, at last, seem worn—
Lie fallen—hands and eyes
Folded—yet, though we mourn and mourn,
A good man never dies.

JAMES WHITCOMB RILEY

O never star
Was lost; here
We all aspire to heaven and there is heaven
Above us.
If I stoop
Into a dark tremendous sea of cloud,
It is but for a time; I press God's lamp
Close to my breast; its splendor soon or late
Will pierce the gloom. I shall emerge some day.

ROBERT BROWNING

We do not believe in immortality because we have proved
it, but we forever try to prove it because we believe it.

JAMES MARTINEAU

As a fond mother, when the day is o'er
Leads by the hand her little child to bed
Half willing, half reluctant to be led,
And leave his broken playthings on the floor,
Still gazing at them through the open door,
Nor wholly reassured and comforted
By promises of others in their stead,
Which, though more splendid, may not please him more;
So Nature deals with us, and takes away

Our playthings one by one, and by hand
Leads us to rest so gently, that we go
Scarce knowing if we wish to go or stay,
Being too full of sleep to understand
How far the unknown transcends the what we know.

HENRY WADSWORTH LONGFELLOW

We pray Thee, O Christ, to keep us under the spell of immortality.

May we never again think and act as if Thou were dead. Let us more and more come to know Thee as a living Lord who hath promised to them that believe: "Because I live, ye shall live also."

Help us to remember that we are praying to the Conqueror of Death, that we may no longer be afraid nor dismayed by the world's problems and threats, since Thou hast overcome the world.

In Thy strong name, we ask for Thy living presence and Thy victorious power. Amen.

PETER MARSHALL

We want to hear from you. Please send your comments about this book
to us in care of the address below. Thank you.

ZondervanPublishingHouse
Grand Rapids, Michigan 49530
http://www.zondervan.com